Plant Spirit Teachings
of
Six Healing Herbs

Book 2 in The Flower Codes series

Heidi Wedd

with Herbal Introductions by
Michelle Carnochan & Pamela Scott

Copyright © Heidi Wedd, Michelle Carnochan & Pamela Scott, 2025

All rights reserved. This book or any portion thereof may not be reproduced or used in any manner whatsoever without the express written permission of the authors.

Published by The Flower Spring

ISBN: 978-1-7635424-2-6 paperback colour
ISBN: 978-1-7635424-4-0 paperback b & w
ISBN: 978-1-7635424-3-3 ebook

Photographs: Heidi Wedd
Cover photo: Niki Kirsten
Cover design: Amy Rose Hewton

Disclaimer: The information in this book is not intended to be used as a substitute for medical advice. Anyone with a medical condition should seek a qualified practitioner.

Table of Contents

Foreword: Rewilding Herbalism 5
The Flower Codes 9
    The Flower Codes Pathway and Sacred Earth Dreaming..12
    The Healing Herb Flower Codes..14
    Working with The Flower Codes 15
    The Flower Code Essences..15
    How to take. 16

Calendula – Divine Masculine..................................... 19
    Herbal Introduction by Pam Scott 20
    Calendula Flower Teachings 22

Dandelion – Rise Rooted 33
    Herbal Introduction by Michelle Carnochan.....................34
    Dandelion Flower Teachings...39

Yarrow - The Beauty of Embodiment......................... 50
    Yarrow Herbal Introduction by Michelle Carnochan 51
    Yarrow Flower Code 55

Chamomile - Inner child 67
    Chamomile Herbal Introduction by Pam Scott 68
    Chamomile Flower Code...72

Rosemary – Divine Feminine 83
    Rosemary Herbal Introduction by Michelle Carnochan...84
    Rosemary Flower Code 88

Mugwort – Great Mother 99
    Mugwort Herbal Introduction by Pam Scott..................100
    Mugwort Teachings 103

Postscript 113
Gratitude 114
Resources... 115
About the Authors 116

Foreword: Rewilding Herbalism

The insights within this book are collated from repeated communications with each herb deva (the soul of the plant). Just as we can't fully know a person from one meeting no matter how deep our interaction is, the inner essence of a plant becomes clearer and more refined the more our relationship with it develops over time.

Engaging in committed, long term relationships with plants - where we learn, evolve and grow together is a pathway to rewilding herbalism. Like any relationship, the exchange is mutual. Getting to know the core essence of a plant is a true gift that we can offer to the plant realm when we take this time. Far from simply knowing its actions and properties, and using its many gifts (cooking, medicinal, practical etc.), when we come to know and work with a plant at the level of its soul essence, the plant shines. The herb's true gift is revealed and *received.* There is nothing quite like being really *seen* after all! Seen not only for its looks, its work in the world, its place in the community, but for who it really is underneath all of that.

Our witnessing of a herb's essence, its eternal essential nature, brings a quality of enlivening - like a spark of vitality - to the plant that helps the plant shine brighter and flourish.

When we go beyond the material and acknowledge the source of the outer effects it may have, we enrich and strengthen the inner realm. This not only serves the individual herb soul, but is felt throughout nature. In effect it is a gift back to the Earth for all that we receive from it.

It is my hope that more people will begin to foster a deeper exploration of the wondrous world of herbs and plant spirit communication, and slowly begin to really *know* plants as the vast wisdom holders they are.   Let's rewild herbalism!

This book contains six of the healing herbs - plants that contain healing teachings that virtually everyone in the world could benefit from in the current era.

The herbal wisdom within these pages comes from:
- *Direct communication with each herb over time.*
  Occasionally I've augmented this with pieces backed up by my own herbal training or herbal experience. On top of these communications, I've been able to refine these themes further and confirm the core essences via:
- *Spagyric alchemy groupwork.*
  Working in a group with a plant allows common themes to become more obvious and extra layers of insight to unfold. Each person's unique resonances, patterns and knowledge adds a different facet so a more holistic and communal focus to a plant's core essence is revealed, allowing the refinement or sometimes broadening, of the themes it carries.
- *My herbal students/colleagues*
  After working with these healing herbs solo or in

alchemy, I've had the pleasure of facilitating shamanic herbalism explorations with these healing herbs as the teachers. Witnessing the processes of countless student/colleagues as they listen deeply and intentionally explore these herbs, has enabled me to clarify and refine the core themes further. It has also been very gratifying to see repeated themes emerge in a plant's teachings *before* I've shared what they are in class!

Within each herb, you will find a comprehensive summary of the herb's folklore, history and medicinal uses written by two knowledgeable herbalists: Pam and Michelle, both plant whisperers in their own right. This is followed by a summary that I have written of the core themes (thus far) of each herb. You can read more about my background and journey with herbs, alchemy, shamanism and plant spirit communication in Book 1 of the Flower Codes series.

You'll notice obvious overlaps across some of the herbs in this book. The more I've explored plant spirit teachings, it becomes ever clearer that *all* plants have a deep underlying theme of *connection* that they can support us with. It seems obvious in retrospect, after all, plants *live* in constant communion and connection with the natural world. Yet each has their different flavour, and so even when you notice overlaps between herbs, it is beneficial to grasp the different expressions they bring to the common teaching. In this way, you can better choose the resonant herb to work with. While all of the herbs in this book are big healers and could be worked with often, it is good practice to learn to discern the individualities of each. Practicing getting to know a herb as a *whole* picture as opposed to simply one action, indication or theme is an integral part of rewilding herbalism.

The Flower Codes

Every flower has a unique vibration or code; a teaching; an essence that it carries through its whole being. To tune into the depths of a plant is to understand this message.

When you meet a person for the first time, you learn a little about them – maybe their name, where they're from etc. Even should you have a deeply intimate conversation with them, there's only so much you can know at one meeting.

Plants are the same.

Relationships with them take time. Information comes out in layers. Even how easily they connect is unique to each plant, just as it is with people.

Herbs are a great place to begin the cocreation journey, as people have had conversations and interactions with herbs for centuries. The relationship has already been cultivated, though there is always more to learn. Plants evolve alongside humanity. If we go purely by old knowledge, we will miss much of their relevance and healing gifts in the *now*. This is one reason developing skills of deep listening and direct, embodied wisdom of a plant is so important. With herbs, there is already a paved pathway to communion, making the process easier. On the other hand, there are plants in the bush that feel as if talking to humans is so far in their distant memories, they've forgotten how to commune with us as much as humanity as a collective has with them. These plants take a little longer to work with.

Making herbal alchemical spagyrics is a great way to deepen with a plant as you are working in depth and sharing a transformative process with the plant. What I have found after countless alchemical adventures with different plants within groups, is that at a certain point in the alchemy, the themes becomes collective. Generally (there are always exceptions to the rule), people receive bits and pieces from the plant's emanation. Different people pick up different information and themes begin to emerge. This continues as the layers of the plant emerge and are shared via communicating with the plant and experiencing the process through the alchemical vessel that is the group field.

At some point, the themes begin to coalesce and everything begins to make sense. This is when you get to the core or soul of the plant, its essential nature or essence, its unique teaching. Once you understand this, all the myriad different symptoms, insights and peripheral actions begin to make sense as you have touched its core essence and can see *why* it works in certain ways (see diagram). In this series, I am focusing on sharing the themes within the core essence.

When I began working with the flower codes (as *they* called themselves) many years ago, they spoke to me of awakening our DNA. At the time, I had no understanding of what this actually meant, though now it has become common in our language. They also shared with me that in times long before ours, this information was much more accessible. By simply smelling a flower, its "code" would be awakened within us. We would open up to an understanding or way of being that this flower was keeper of. While this knowledge was slowly forgotten over time, remnants remain within us. Throughout history, there have always been those who held herbal lore and wisdom and the ability to unlock a plants wisdom strands and activate it in another - sometimes simply by placing the flower in their psychic field.

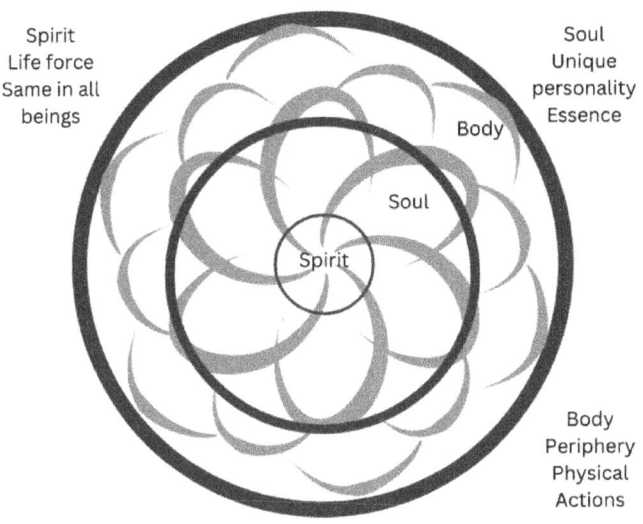

While we are not quite back at that state of being, the flower codes are coming back into consciousness now for a reason – because we are ready to come back to that state of awareness again. That is the intention of these particular flowers and their teachings - to reawaken and help us remember this way of being.

Flowers *were* and *are* a language.
Each has a unique vibration.
The flower codes activate specific states of being within us. They are like archetypal energies, simple and divine.

Activating and embodying these natural states of being within ourselves, reawakens them on the Earth.

The Flower Codes Pathway and Sacred Earth Dreaming

There are (so far) nine core flower codes or "portal flowers." Each of these is a gateway into a whole realm creating a pathway spelt out in the language of flowers.

What has slowly revealed itself in connecting with these nine central flowers is that they can help us remember the *original* coding of a Sacred Earth reality or consciousness. The best I can explain this state of being from the glimpses I have experienced, is a world in which everything (plants, animals, mountains, lakes, elementals etc.) is considered sacred, where every action takes into account the whole because the effect is felt immediately throughout oneself. It is an indigenous state of being. Separation is an illusion most of us currently exist in. In this connected space, each unique flower can be felt and experienced directly and immediately.

These core flower codes or portals support us to remember and reawaken this way of being, something that lies dormant within us. By engaging with these plants, we can begin to embody a Sacred Earth consciousness.

In all truly holistic healing, we heal from the centre out, focusing not on symptoms but on deep cause. (see image). With the flower codes we do the same - we begin by activating our true and natural state - our unique essence. When we work with any of the nine portal flowers, we begin touching on these natural states within.

As we do this, what often arises is how far we have transgressed away from our natural essence or sacred earth state. Wounds arise and the need for healing may appear.

The Healing Herb flowers within this book fit in the category of *supportive allies* to the central flowers.

As an example, within the first three flowers (see Book 1), we are remembering birth as a sacred portal, the blueprint of its best expression as an initiation and gateway into the physical realm. However, an enormous percentage of people on the planet have not experienced birth in this way, instead experiencing interruption or trauma. While the core flowers of Sacred Birth help us to remember what is possible and provide this subtle assistance, there are times when we may need to use *healing herb* flowers to clear the trauma and wounding - Calendula, Bellis, Hypericum, Yarrow are a few examples (there's no coincidence that these are some of the biggest birth trauma remedies!) Working firstly with the core flowers, yet calling in healing herbs as needed, we begin to reweave our own DNA and neural imprinting, the earthly strands we are embedded within, along with the Earth itself.

The Healing Herb Flower Codes

This category within the flower codes framework consists of twelve herbs whose healing capacity is both personal and collective. These are herbs that basically anyone living today could benefit from at various times, and for the most part, quite often. They grow all over the world and are well known everyday herbs - many of them common in the culinary sphere. This is a plant signature in itself - they are *collective herbal healers* - herbs of great use for humanity.

Nature always provides.

Mythically, the healing herbs sprang forth when our sacred connection to nature began to falter. They are here to support us to heal the wounds and traumas that accompanied this loss and disconnect. Like balms for the soul, when we lose our balance, nature creates a pathway of healing. There is a plant for every purpose.

The healing herbs can bridge the gaps between us and the central flower codes. They make great supportive aids alongside them and are also epic healers in their own right.

Working with The Flower Codes

There are a myriad of ways to awaken the flower code teachings within us. Conscious work with the themes below, along with immersing yourself in the field of the flower is all that is required.

The Flower Code essences are an easy way in. Because many of them contain spagyric tinctures made in true alchemical form (deep communion and cocreation with the plant in an evolutionary process between both the plant and those making it), they carry an updated or evolved version of the plant so hold the medicine to get you quickly up to speed in the unique area of wisdom they cover.

For a deeper and wholistic immersion you can join the *Flower Codes Training*, in which we develop communications with the plant and work with their teachings in order to fully activate and embody them within us.

The Flower Code Essences

The Flower Codes are similar yet different to flower essences. While they are completely safe and can be taken in the same way as flower essences, their action and intention are slightly different. They work to activate and remember states of consciousness within us, and contain a cocreated and *evolved* form of the flower. Because they have been 'evolved' through the co-creative process with the flower, some of the work is already done for you. However, it is always better to work consciously alongside the plant on the themes you need assistance with. This enables deeper healing and a recognition of the inner processes involved.

Each flower code is made using specific instructions in conversation with each plant deva, hence each process is different and unique to the flower. Some are pure flower essences activated with sound; others are a combination of spagyrics, flower essences and homeopathic potencies blended over a certain period of time, at a specific time of the year, with sound, intention and devic activation. They are made when the devas say the time is ripe, so not all have been made to this point in time.

How to take.

The general suggestion is to take the drops 2-3 times a day over a 3-5 week period. However, this should be tempered with your own knowing and feeling. Take as needed and if you feel to stop, stop. Come back when you are ready.

Before you start, set an intention or journal around why you have chosen this essence. Then over the weeks you are taking it, check in and journal regularly as to what is arising, and shifting in you. Engage in the process for a more potent shift in the activation process.

Use your intuition and inner knowing. Maybe a flower has called you or has shown up in your life. Trust that and start there. If in doubt, start with the portal flowers - Feverfew is the beginning of the pathway.

The supporting flower code groups are allies to assist with what arises when working with the core flowers. There is a reason they are common herbs found around the world – most people can benefit from them!

Calendula – Divine Masculine

Calendula Officinalis
Asteraceae

Calendula

Herbal Introduction by Pam Scott

Other names: Curl Flower, Rampant Flower, Bride of the Sun, Summers Bride, Husband's Dial, Gold Flower of Mary, Herb of the Sun.

It is thought the name Calendula is derived from "calends" as the Romans believed it bloomed every calendar month or possibly with each new moon.

As a native to Southern Europe and Asia, it is a tough self-seeding annual that grows up to about 50cm high with yellow or orange daisy-like flowers. The soft, long and slightly sticky leaves alternate on the stem. It flowers all through summer and into autumn depending on the climate in the area. A lover of full sun, it can be happy in partial shade. It prefers a well-drained soil and the seeds can be planted directly into the garden, though it doesn't do well in the frosty cold.

In earlier times Calendula was looked upon as a rain indicator. If the flowers were still closed at 7am then it would rain or storm that day. Others observed them opening at 9am and closing at 3pm as if they were following the sunshine.

Harvest flowers in the heat of the day and dry quickly in a well ventilated, dark place.

There are many superstitions around Calendula depending on where you are in the world. It is a popular ingredient in charms and spells that may give a maiden an insight or a dream into who they may marry. In India, garlands of Calendula are still very much used in wedding ceremonies. To hang it in your doorway or scatter the petals around your bed, it will protect you from evil. It is a Christian symbol for salvation after death. It denotes eternal life, and in Mexico and Germany it is associated with death.

One of the myths of Calendula is of the four wood nymphs that were in love with the sun god Apollo. Their jealousies distracted them from looking after Apollo's sister, the goddess Diana. She retaliated by turning them into four white marigolds. Apollo was distressed but all he could do was to send down his golden rays to colour them.

In folklore it is known as 'herbal sunshine' as the flowers appear to represent the sun and have been used to bring relief and lift the spirits from dark and depressive states. "It brings joy and great sunshine to the heart and mind."

Medicinally it has been used for wounds, glandular and lymphatic conditions. The flowers were put in soups and stews to relieve sluggish lymphatic conditions and long-term infections before, during and after winter. It is also considered an immune tonic.

The active principles of Calendula excel in activating and cleaning wounds and grazes of debris, pus and inflammation. It increases the proliferation of cells and the granulation of the wounded area. Anywhere where there is damaged tissue and slow healing wounds, Calendula helps seal off blood vessels, aids torn tissue and restores nerve function. It is used successfully for measles, chickenpox, ulcers, blisters, bites, acne and for places 'where the sun don't shine' such as nappy rash and haemorrhoids. It heals with no or minimal scarring.

Its bitter components improve the digestive process, sluggish bowels and gaseous conditions as well as congested pelvic regions. It is antispasmodic and could open up and relieve some menstrual conditions such as dysmenorrhea and amenorrhea

Constituents: Volatile oils, mucilage, resins, saponins, carotenoids, bitters, flavonoids, sterols, calendulin, polysaccharides.

Actions: Antifungal, bacteriostatic, anti-inflammatory, styptic, antispasmodic, antiseptic, aperient, diaphoretic, cholagogue, febrifuge, vulnerary, stimulant, emmenagogue.

Contraindications: When taken internally it may stimulate bile flow and could awaken a sluggish liver too effectively producing biliousness. Avoid during pregnancy although it would be fine topically. (NB. Calendula Flower Code essence can be used at any time).

Calendula Flower Teachings

Most people know Calendula as a great healer for surface wounds, grazes, tooth infections, nipple balm and re-granulating tissue trauma. As an antiseptic it prevents the spread of infection and heals open wounds beautifully. It's long been known as a remedy to bring cheer through a long winter (Seasonally Affective Disorder), and to bring a little dose of sunshine to any rotting tissues that are lacking light and need warming, drying, soothing and purifying. But Calendula goes much deeper than that. Like most common herbs, there is an epic need for them in our culture. They grow amidst us patiently waiting to be embraced as the deep teachers and healers that they are - when we are ready to look below the surface level.

Calendula, as one of the healing herb flower codes, is a big one as it covers all the wounding inflicted by an unintegrated, unhealed inner masculine (irrespective of gender or identification). In a long history of abusive patriarchal behaviour in which the feminine (and women as representative) have been raped and dismissed rather than integrated and respected, the need for Calendula is rife. The constant pillaging of the Earth without care for its creatures, plants and the Earth's sentience, is another aspect of this that is still very much in effect today.

We are at a time in our evolution where the inner masculine needs to be looked at for deep healing. The wounds both inflicted and received through disrespect and dishonouring of the inner feminine need to be reopened and healed properly. Calendula is a huge support in this process, from the recent to the ancient. Whether it is dealing with domestic violence, old wounds inflicted by the wounded masculine, institutions that don't honour the feminine, lost wisdom, violence towards the earth, or whether it is driving our bodies beyond healthy limits, the time to heal the masculine is nigh. For at the core of Calendula, lies the wound of separation and division – the source of wars, battles, conflicts and competition.

Gold, Sun, Light, Heart.
Calendula with its golden solar blooms that open and close with the sun throughout the year, is a beautiful plant signature of the sun. It whispers to us of themes around light, gold, warmth, fire and radiance.

In Greek myth, a water nymph *Clytie*, fell in love with the sun god *Helios* (in later versions it was *Apollo* - a more recent sun deity). Yet he was unmoved by her and Clytie was left following his glory adoringly across the sky in the heights of unrequited love. Until eventually the gods took pity on her and after nine days, turned her into a flower - variously mentioned as a heliotrope, sunflower or Calendula, who continues to trace the path of the sun across the sky day after day.

Just as the sun is central to the solar system, the King is central to the people. A good king like Calendula, has a heart of gold. Gold has a purity that can withstand incredible forces without being tarnished. It stays true to itself like a healthy Calendula archetype. Yet when it is not balanced within us, we can see the unmoved and uncaring aspect that Clytie experiences in her own reflection.

Calendula's central theme is the *Divine Masculine* – the healthy or healed masculine, a theme we will return to.

Like gentle fire in the body, Calendula helps to build our basic warmth and vital force. This solar, more yang or masculine energy creates an energetic movement towards the periphery - outwards and upwards. Like an inner sun, it warms, purifies and clears dampness and stagnancy. For stagnant lymph or swollen lymph glands, lowered immunity, and wounds that keep getting wet, think of Calendula.

Yet we mustn't forget that while the flower opens and shines during the day, at night it closes and goes inwards. Day and night, light and dark. While Calendula works with dampness and stagnancy, if we are too hot and dry, it can bring nourishment, soothing and grounding to irritated tissue and burns. Plants are beautiful like that. They have intelligence and can work with what needs to happen if we have a deeper knowledge and relationship with them. Calendula is able to seamlessly blend supposed opposites as well as it sews the two sides of torn tissue back together.

As an energetic heart medicine, Calendula radiates warmth and a light full of love. The healthy Calendula within, radiates and glows from the inner core outward. This radiance shines brightly but with a soft, loving and gentle kindness to it - a result of its integration with the polar feminine or watery qualities.

Calendula also has a relationship to light and helps us to integrate sunlight properly, soothing the physical burns of sunlight (sunburn) as well as the more internal spiritual ones. Deeper still, it helps to build our inner light and balance that with external solar light. It broadens our capacity to shine our own light and build our inner gold radiance. It will shine light into the darkest, blackest and festering places within us that may be stopping us from emanating our radiance. This warmth, light and awareness helps to cleanse, purify, heal and re-granulate inner wounds - even if they have been held within us for centuries or within the memories of our ancestry. Like sunlight it pours in healing energy that soothes the physical *and* the emotional burns and wounds, especially those inflicted by the unhealed masculine.

The Divine Masculine
Calendula holds the coding for the divine masculine or divine father energy. When working with Calendula flower code, whatever is lying between us experiencing and expressing our own divine masculine may arise to be cleared. It is a BIG wound medicine.

Before we go into ways that the wounded masculine can play out, let's look at the divine masculine in its healthy form.

The greatest teaching and message from Calendula is that the masculine cannot be 'divine' or 'healed' unless it has *integrated the feminine.*

The healed masculine is integrated with the feminine knowing there is no separation, they are two parts of a whole. *The healed masculine is never masculine alone.* It can't be healed AND separate. Understanding this wisdom and embodying it is an epic collective mission in our current day!

An archetype of the Healed/Divine Masculine could be that of the middle age Knight in Shining Armour who protects, supports and fights for the feminine from a place of deep respect and honour for her. This is a healthy masculine who honours the body, the Earth and the feminine as external counterparts. Who understands sensitivity and fragility and is pledged to protect and honour that, for it knows the deep creative power of the inner feminine and that existence rests on its protection.

The healthy masculine radiates a divine light that is filled with love and softened by compassion. The *Divine Father energy* is like the caring love of a father, which softens the pure masculine energy and integrates it.

Calendula teaches that you can't separate the masculine and feminine without causing deep wounds. It helps us remember the unity - that masculine and feminine exist together, that they are two sides of a single coin. It is nourishing and healing for the neural pathways and balances left and right hemispheres of the brain. Calendula helps reunite and remember that there is no real separation. It works towards this, speaking to the core human wound of separation and division. It helps to create balance and harmony in relationship by addressing any wounds that block the way.

Working with the inner masculine to heal the wounds within the soul is potent activism for the planet. As we learn to shine our light with love, rather than burning without a care for *all* others, our hearts shine like gold and radiate with joy.

The wounded masculine
In the recent herstory/history of patriarchy, Calendula coding can bring up a lot of past wounding that has sat quietly festering in the bloodlines below the surface of our awareness for centuries. It shines light in order to purify and cleanse, preventing the further spread of infection along the ancestral lines.

The unhealed masculine within, may show up in so many ways: toxic masculinity; father wounds; a desire to dominate others; being dominated by others; cruelty; lack of feeling and compassion towards others, animals or plants; dismissal of emotions or of physical needs; shutdown of emotions; 'pushing beyond' to the detriment of the body (use of painkillers, excessive exertion, eating unhealthy food in excess); the desire to achieve to the detriment of the body; not respecting the need to play, process, rest or simply *be;* disconnection between head and heart; intellect over body, or mind over matter to detriment; the using of nature for our own desires without listening to her needs or giving back; abuse of the physical body and its subtle needs; current agricultural, hospital and pharmaceutical systems; competitiveness; sisterhood wounds and so many more.

Calendula will quite literally shine light on these ways within us when immersing in its soul medicine.

Working with Calendula flower code has seen many a memory of collective wounds against the feminine and women. One may catch glimpses of the mutilation, rape and murder of women throughout time. Whether playing the role of victim or inflictor, both have created deep seated wounding in the collective psyche. Calendula gently shows us that the reason these horrific events have occurred throughout history is due to a disconnect. The wound of separation. As perpetrators we are able to inflict such horror onto other beings due to being cut off from the inner feminine. It is a deep schism that makes us capable of being able to harm another without feeling. For in order to kill, a separation or a disconnect from the feeling realm is required.

Calendula is for when we are subtly over identified with the masculine, for when we have separated from the feminine, disconnected with the earth or are in the field of separation in general. It helps purify the wounds created from this and re-granulate these two parts of one whole back into union.

Mind over matter.
This is a theme in Calendula and another echo of the above. The separation between the head and the body, the rational and feeling, masculine and feminine. *Mind over matter* says it all. Not mind *with* matter, but *over*. This is mirrored out in the collective as decapitations, beheadings, the throat being cut or severed – all images that came through working with Calendula. After working in depth with Calendula, I feel the sadness of Clytie when I see people topping the flower heads of Calendula rather than listening to how it would love to be

picked. After all, the Calendula petals will show you when they are offering themselves as they will start to separate themselves from the head, beautifully sun dried and ready for medicine. This also allows the head to form seeds and continue its life cycle. If you are needing the green head, whole leaves and stem for its resins, then picking at the joint is a loving, connected and more respectful way of working with *any* plant. The unhealed masculine is so deeply ingrained in western culture that it can take a lot of slowing down, tuning in, and noticing when we are *doing to* rather than *working with*.

Not taking care of the physical body with sensitivity is another way this rift can play out. When we are using the body (or the Earth) for our own agendas, rather than listening to the needs (of our body or the Earth), we are in unhealthy patterns of domination and control. The healed masculine on the other hand, knows how to listen and respect the needs of the body and the Earth and work *with* them.

Doing and being.
The masculine and feminine right? That's what I thought too. Again, Calendula showed me how deeply ingrained the unhealthy, unintegrated masculine is in our belief systems. Calendula threw this concept right out for me. The divine masculine doesn't need to "do," he just "is". *Doing* is an aspect of the unhealed, the need to control, the pushing through energy, force. Integrated *action* on the other hand, arises from simply being. It comes from within.

Once you work through the surface level wounds, you begin to get to the deeper wounds of separation and here the great paradox of Calendula teaching unfolds - *even separating the mind from the body is an ingrained wound of separation.* Calendula eventually teaches how all opposing forces, dark and light, up and down, masculine and feminine, etc. are simply two sides of the same coin. Take one side away and wholeness is lost. The warring between any poles, is ultimately ridiculous. Once you begin to clear the wounds of separation, this becomes so clear.

The distortion of herbs and nature. Reknitting wounds in the fabric of creation.
Calendula is like running sunshine through your veins, which like gold, helps to release impurities. A very important message that Calendula shared is its capacity to help us release imprinted information regarding our body's capacity to receive from plants and nature. It awakens our body's capacity to process Earth in all her dimensional realities.

Another wound Calendula helps to shine light on in order to heal, is the distortion of the authentic blueprint of herbs and their power. This is a schism that has slowly unfolded through the ages due to numerous events like the slow disrespecting and disregard for the Earth as a being, the age of patriarchal influence, the killing of healers and herbalists, witch hunts, and on and on right down to the current influence of pharmaceutical companies dominating the 'healing' sector and the unhealthy ways people choose to *use* herbs rather than *cocreating* and *working with* them. Further still, distortions in the properties of healing plants can be apparent.

Calendula can help us to clear these influences from within us so that we can remember a time when healing herbs were loved, tended and cocreated with by all. It can help us uncover and receive the authentic blueprints of herbs without all the distorted imprinted information layered on top. To know a herb in its true form directly.

Calendula in Summary
Calendula helps balance the strength of the solar masculine energy with the feminine receptive and feeling realms, bringing warmth and caring into the mix. Ultimately, Calendula activates the healthy inner masculine - that which is integrated with the feminine.

Calendula at its core holds the coding for the divine masculine. As a healing herb it has the ability to bring this about again by healing ancient unhealed wounds. It cuts open old psychological scars and deep black wounds in order to shine light on them so that they may heal properly. It brings wounds to the surface for deep healing. Just as it is a balm for the skin, nappy rash, wounds, etc. Calendula is a balm for the soul. *It assists the reknitting of fractals, wounds and light frequencies displaced during timeline corruptions.*[1] It clears blockages to receiving, opening us to allow the light of transformation in again. It helps to restore trust in the feminine and the body again.

It has the potency to heal our ancestral lines as well as current wounds. Like all herbs, Calendula will work with where you're at. If there are ancient stagnant wounds to be cleared in the bloodlines, this is what it will tend, softly bringing them to the surface and like a balm, easing and soothing their release while bringing consciousness to them.

---

[1] Words received from a participant communing with Calendula during alchemical spagyric making experience.

It heals by running its golden energy through the blood and the bloodlines, purifying them. It strengthens the auric field and our ability to sense and recognise threats, protect ourselves and strengthens our resilience.

Beyond this it can go even further - soul reclaiming, reconnection, true wholeness, true divine nature in active wholeness and taking us to layers of 'soul beyond the schism'. Our utter inner radiance. The golden King and Queen who mutually respect each other and live in equality without the need for power plays.

It calls up all that is not aligned within us (e.g. fear and doubt) and moves through the body clearing these blockages so that we can come to a fuller, more enlivened, radiating version of our soul.

Dandelion – Rise Rooted

Taraxacum officinale
Asteraceae

Dandelion

Herbal Introduction by Michelle Carnochan

Presently, it is a cold and wet winter's day, I'm rugged up by the fire, and the aroma from a decoction of raw Dandelion root simmering on the stove is wafting through the house. As I allow my mind to wander and waft with the rich aroma of Dandelion's earthy nourishing sweetness, I can't help but feel my spirit descend beneath the leaf litter into the dark realm of dwarves and gnomes and glowing webs of mycelia, and deep anchoring tree roots below. Intuitively, the cooler seasons are a time for going inward, and for me, infusing my home and soul with the aroma of a Dandelion decoction and then drinking deeply of its medicine has become a ritual synonymous with winter and this introspective process. It is one of my favourite times of the year. It is a time when I embrace the opportunity not only to reflect on the year that's been and the lessons learned and goals achieved, and to think of my ancestors, but it is also when I make time to do the shadow work. Dandelion works with these dark spaces in between, exposing, digesting and transmuting the hidden things into the light, and even in the bleak mid-winter, Dandelion's golden solar-loving blossoms still grace the garden here and there reminding us of this alchemical magic that occurs in both the wheel of the year, and in our body.

A member of the huge Asteraceae/Compositae family, Dandelion is native to Europe and Asia, but has followed people all over the world, where it has naturalised in largely temperate zones, and to the angst of many a fastidious lawn keeper, it grows wherever it desires. Its formidable resilience often sees it grow through cracks in the concrete in the heart of the busiest cities. Its long taproot mines into the earth, aerates the soil and draws up minerals and other vital nutrients. While the smooth, hollow flower stalk shoots up straight and tall from the root, the leaves grow in a basal rosette radiating out from the root crown. The pointed leaf is smooth and hairless with a single mid-rib, the margins are deeply indented and jagged, as if sharply toothed, and the leaf can grow up to 30cm long. The flower stalk remains leafless, bearing only one golden flower per stalk. The hollow stem produces a milky latex when broken, and both the leaf and stem are hairless. The nectar-scented golden composite flower is universally adored by bees. The flower opens and closes in rhythm with the rising and setting sun. When the flower is spent, a seed head forms that reminds me of an ethereal lunar puffball - a white pincushion with lots of tiny gyroscopic seed points. Seeds are dispersed by wind and small wishful children. This puffball was also used to predict the weather as it is sensitive to changes in atmospheric moisture, closing when it is going to rain and opening when it is dry again. The plant blooms all year round, and although only one stem produces one flower, it is common to see a plant with a number of stems with flower or seed head growing from the one plant at the same time.

This mining, aerating taproot, and subsequent mineral-rich leaves do the same in us, clearing away stagnancy, stuckness and congestion and the heat it generates, and encouraging a fresh, cooling flow in the digestive processes of both body and mind. The root is primarily associated with the liver, the leaves with the kidneys. The golden flower speaks to the solar plexus. In Traditional Chinese Medicine, these organs are associated with stuck anger and fear, and lack of or overactive willpower respectively. Dandelion helps us to explore the root cause of these stagnant emotions and help move them on and motivate us in healthier ways. Dandelion has an affinity for the whole digestive process through a specific affinity for the liver, gallbladder, pancreas, colon, the kidneys, the interstitial fluid, as well as breast tissue, and is therefore a helpful ally in dealing with the specific issues that each of these organs may suffer. It also influences bone, teeth enamel, and connective tissue due to its high mineral content and improved absorption and assimilation in the digestive process. The flowers infused in oil make a wonderful breast massage oil and relieve muscular tension wherever it is needed.

One of the most curious indications for dandelion is the 'geographic tongue'. Patches of a thick white sticky covering on the tongue come away exposing the red raw layers of flesh underneath giving the tongue a 'mapped' look. It occurs due to congested heat in the liver, which dandelion cools and disperses. Overall, dandelion is a powerful but gentle detoxifier and tonic. Culpeper says that Dandelion is '*of an opening and cleansing quality.*' The milky latex has a long history of use on warts.

All parts of the plant can be used as medicine in all the ways that herbal medicines are prepared, as well as a nourishing food in dishes such as soups, salads, and to make beer, wine, and coffee substitutes. Although if you use the raw root in place of the commercially favoured roasted root in Chai or as a substitute for coffee, for example, then you're probably performing some sort of chaos magic, which according to Scott Cunningham in *The Encyclopaedia of Magical Herbs* says will "*aid divination & prophetic dreaming. [and] leaving the tea to sit by the bedside is said to call spirits."* I concur with this clarifying aspect. The root of a 2-year-old plant unearthed in autumn is believed to hold the best medicine. The young leaves are picked in spring. The flowers picked when blooming. However, the plant can be harvested and worked with at any time the need arises without fear. UK-based Herbalist, Lucy Jones from the Myrobalan Clinic brought to light the use of a tincture of the seed head. She uses it with alternating doses of the tincture of the flower to help bring balance to those suffering from Bipolar. (Here we see the polarity of the flower and the seed head - day and night, sun and moon, yang and yin, masculine and feminine).

To the taste, whether in tea, tincture or raw, the root is earthy, milk-sweet, and has some bitterness. The young tender leaves are slightly bitter and salty to taste, the mature leaves are bitter. The flower has a delicate sweetness and smells divine like honey. In the body, these tastes have both moistening and cooling energies. The whole plant contains sesquiterpene lactones, triterpenes, vitamins A, B, C & D. The leaf contains coumarins, carotenoids, minerals (calcium, magnesium, iron, zinc, chromium, potassium), and bitter glycosides. The root contains choline, glycosides, triterpenes, taraxacoside, minerals, & phenolic acids.

'Dandelion' comes from the French 'dent-de-lion' or 'tooth of the lion' in reference to the leaf, and variations of this name are also found across many of the European languages. It is also called Piss-en-lit (French), Pissabed, Priest's Crown, Swine's Snout, and Blow ball. Both references to wetting the bed allude to the diuretic properties of the leaf, although paradoxically Dandelion has also been used for the very issue of bedwetting due to its high-mineral content. (Dandelion is a potassium-sparing diuretic, giving it a valuable place in also working with congestive heart failure.) As for 'Priest's Crown' and 'Sow's Snout', the origin of these common names is elusive. Blowball refers to the seed head that children have blown throughout time to make wishes and tell the time.

In America, it has historically also been called Cankerwort, meaning 'herb for the canker'. Canker was a term used by the American root doctor Samuel Thomson to describe the lack of fire in the belly and the resulting accumulated toxic matter, much like the concept of Agni (vital digestive fire) and Amma (toxic mucus accumulation) in Ayurvedic medicine. Dandelion's botanical name, *Taraxacum officinale* comes from the Greek '*taraxo*' & '*achos*' meaning 'disorder' & 'remedy' respectively. '*Officinale*' refers to plants included in the catalogue of official medicines.

As a valuable source of food and medicine, dandelion has an ancient written record of use dating back to the ancient Egyptians, Greeks, and Romans, through to references in the ancient texts of Ayurveda and Traditional Chinese Medicine, and from European Medieval references up to the present day. However, we can assume that it was also used long before written records began. It is evident that it also has a history of use amongst cultures where it was introduced. American herbalist Gail Faith Edwards lists no less than eight Native American tribes who used Dandelion for various ailments in varying preparations. J.T Garrett in 'The Cherokee Herbal' places Dandelion as a West Medicine in the Cherokee Medicine Wheel. Plants of the West are considered 'animal medicines,' intended to restore a person's physical strength and endurance.

Culpeper says it is ruled by Jupiter. In some traditions it is also associated with the solar deities, and in Finnish folklore it is associated with the sun.

When I drink my decoction in this place of deep winter reflection I am comforted by Dandelion's medicine. Resilient and strong, it stands in its power knowing that it represents the alchemical process of transformation. It is not afraid, because it knows that all things hidden will be brought to the light, and then can be healed and so this becomes wisdom. What was once bitter becomes sweet.

Dandelion Flower Teachings

Dandelion is one of the healing herb flower codes and in its magnanimousness, could easily be taken regularly by just about everyone to great benefit. As an all-round liver herb, it supports the processing of emotions and toxins and the smooth flow of energy throughout the body so that we can be *hollow stems*, deeply grounded and from there, rise rooted. From the words of Dandelion itself - it is not a *one-time plant*, rather something to be taken regularly over time. So let's look at some of Dandelion's themes and core teachings.

Grounding, anchoring, rooted.
It's rare, tuning into Dandelion, to not feel a deeper sense of grounding. Dandelion has a low centre of gravity - the leaves begin just underground, its centre rising from within the earth rather than above it. In the same way, it helps us to

drop into *our* centre of gravity as well as ground deeply into our roots. For those who don't often reside here, it can bring a real sense of solidity as we relax into the core of our being to find there is no reason to force things. When we are anchored in ourselves, all action arises naturally. For those who have a tendency to push, force or control, Dandelion brings us back into the core, anchoring and grounding so there is no need to try so hard. Dandelion will show you where you rise out of your centre and are not fully grounded in your actions. For those who live or move from their heads, Dandelion can tangibly bring a felt experience of what it feels to be grounded in the earth and connected with your central core.

Rise rooted
When we are grounded in both our roots and our core, any upward motion is firmly anchored and hence strong, resilient and able to withstand whatever life throws at us. For those who rise too fast without a firm anchoring, Dandelion encourages us to anchor back down, to find our roots and the nutrients we need to grow tall. Alternatively, for those who easily become stuck in the mud and a little *too* anchored, Dandelion helps to rise, open, clear and grow upwards.

Dandelion has a beautiful affinity for the earth elementals - the gnomes, and you may catch a glimpse of them while exploring Dandelion energetically. Like most herbs, the polar elemental will also be at play - in this case the air element, where we see its rising, expansive movement and the starry heads of the seeds spreading far. Dandelion demonstrates the beauty of harmony between the two - how we expand and grow further, the deeper our roots. When we attempt to expand without strong foundations, longevity is short. Dandelion has existed for aeons and knows this! A survivor of many an abuse, it can help us overcome abusive situations of our own, transmuting it into healthy resilience without getting stuck or holding onto old traumas and abuses. It supports us to rise rooted.

Liver and Smooth Flow

Dandelion with its yellow flower is an all-round gentle liver tonic as well as supporting the kidneys in excretion. On a broad spectrum, the liver is the body's processor - it processes the blood, distributing incoming food and energies to where they need to go, and clearing toxins or packaging them for safe storage. In Chinese medicine, the liver has a number of functions not recognised by western medicine, yet they explain much of what arises when working with the Dandelion deva. One of these functions of the liver is the smooth flow of qi/energy throughout the body. Thus if the liver is not functioning well, stuckness, stagnation and build-up become apparent.

Dandelion is particularly useful when we are stuck, blocked or stagnant in any way. 'Taraxis' (of *Taraxacum)* may also stem from the Greek *tarach* meaning 'to stir up or disturb,' referring to its power to stimulate and get things moving. *Ataraxia*, its opposite, is a state of tranquillity and unperturbability. Dandelion contains both these qualities - the ability to get things moving when they are backed up, yet also the strength of character that, like the Dandelion plant, can withstand constant tests - being trodden on, weeded out and historically demeaned, yet it has survived somewhat *unperturbed* throughout the ages, nonetheless.

When there is a build-up of rubbish, toxins or baggage, whether physical or emotional - or whether you're in need of a general detox, Dandelion is a gentle, long-term champion. Grumpiness, ill humour, toxicity and liverish symptoms such as irritation, sneezing, allergies or tension headaches may all be a sign of liver overload. Personally, I keep a small bottle of Dandelion tincture by my bed for those times when I may have overindulged in rich food or a glass of alcohol and suspect my liver will rebel overnight. Three drops before bed prevents me from receiving a toxic liver headache by giving the liver that little extra support. Or should I wake between 1-3am (liver time) with the start of a liver headache, if I take a couple of drops of Dandelion tincture, by morning all is well.

In this day and age, our livers are constantly overloaded with all that they need to process. As well as the foods we eat, the emotions we experience and the hormones that need breaking down, the liver must now add to that the processing of massive amounts of external stimulation, pesticides, radiation, screen use and countless other modern-day side effects. Thus, Dandelion is a herb that most people can take constantly to deal with the overload of energies that our livers may struggle to process, simply from sheer excess, leaving us clogged up. A daily cup of Dandelion root 'coffee' or dandelion leaf tea can be basic liver maintenance in today's hectic world.

Motion, Growth, Wood and Anger
As well as the smooth flow of qi, the liver rules the muscles. Commonly for people tuning in with Dandelion comes a strong desire to move, stretch or dance. With an

accompanying sense that body tension needs to *move* or *be moved* out of the muscles.

Tense neck and shoulders, mild tension headaches, stiff jaw and neck and an underlying tension that builds to toxicity were all very apparent on a month-long spagyric group process with Dandelion.

It is through motion that we shift and clear toxins stored throughout the body, to keep them moving through us rather than stuck in the tissues. This is Dandelion medicine. Dandelion absolutely loves to move and dance in circles and cycles, clearing from the centre outwards.

The liver is the yin organ of the Wood element in the Chinese five element system. The Wood element relates to the upwards and outwards motion of Spring and growth (overlapping with Air in the four-element system). The emotion of Wood is anger - another Dandelion theme. When in balance, anger is simply an expression of the strong and directed outward energy that is needed to expand and move forwards.

Growth.

Like the Wood element, Dandelion has an expansive quality that can manifest in both gluttonous excess or an expansion of spirits. Likewise, it purifies the excesses and supports the removal of toxins that may be a result of any unhealthy abundances.

Liver/wood imbalances that result in muscular tension, spasms or headaches - especially in the neck and shoulders, can well need Dandelion to balance out the flow of energy.

Stagnation, Clear vessel, Root cause, Detox

Dandelion holds the deeper teaching that if things are getting stuck, to look to the sticky part. As root medicine, Dandelion guides us to look to the *root cause,* so as to create lasting change. When we heal from the centre, we're looking to the *core issue, the root cause,* not simply the superficial level. Dandelion is purifying and nourishing at the same time and works particularly on the innermost levels of our being - the yin areas. It can help us to find and clear deep-seated patterning by getting to the root cause.

It supports us to discover the resonant pattern, feeling, story, belief, ("sticky bit") that is attracting residue. The build-up of residue blocks the smooth flow of energy. Without this build up, anything not to our benefit would pass right through and be excreted.

Dandelion's hollow stem is a beautiful healthy plant signature for its capacity to propel from the centre outwards and promote being a *clear vessel.* When we are a clear vessel, all can pass through without getting stuck. Like a healthy digestive system, we absorb what we require and release the rest. It is only when there's a "sticky bit" that residue gathers and builds. Dandelion flower code is to help us work towards being a clear vessel, to allow any mud to flow through and out the other side. To attend to the sticky bits.

Emotionally, it is no different. When emotions are not freely *moving* through us (via healthy processing), they become stuck. The resulting strain on the liver - our emotional processor and purifier - can lead to toxin build up and eventually overflow.

Dandelion is a *redistributor* of energies in the body and also in the Earth. Where there is stagnancy or build up, it redistributes substances. Dandelion is one of Earth's great

healers - it moves around to grow in compacted, damaged land, where it helps to de-compact soil and draw up precious minerals from the deep to remineralise the soil. It works the same way in our body, (e.g. the remineralisation of teeth when they have been *undermined*) by redistributing precious minerals where they are needed. Again, we see Dandelion's affinity with the gnomes who work the magic in our physical bodies (earth element) as well as in the soil of the outer Earth (by detoxing heavy metals and redistributing minerals). Dandelion is a plant that functions as a liver for the Earth.

At a deeper level, Dandelion also speaks of the redistribution of energy and resources globally which would bring more equality and balance. As it highlights blockages, this remains a current global issue that Dandelion wishes to make us more aware of - the smooth flow of resources between people is currently blocked and backed up and in need of a good cleanse and rebalance.

Addictions

Dandelion particularly works with addictions, helping bring awareness to our patterns of addiction and where they stem from, so that we can begin to address them at the root rather than with a subtle or obvious addiction. Not only are addictions a common way of suppressing what is arising, they are also a circular pattern that we become stuck in - both very Dandelion themes. Whether it is an addiction to shopping, alcohol, drugs, exercise, relationships, coffee, chocolate or anything else - when we are using it to push down our feelings, the extra pressure on the liver leads to a build-up of toxins and blockages in our system. Even the 'healthiest' of addictions sets up an unhealthy brain chemistry over time. Dandelion shows us how it is not the substance that is always doing harm, but the unprocessed and stagnant emotions that slowly accrete in the body and cause toxicity.

Addictions put a heavy strain on the liver – not simply the more obvious alcohol and drug addictions that result in hepatitis or liver cirrhosis, but also the more subtle ones.

Dandelion can help us get to the root of deep-seated addictions and be present to what is going on rather than run away or look to create a different feeling through a substance or action. To feel exactly whatever it is that feels uncomfortable so that it can move through us and be healthily processed by the liver, allows us to absorb the teaching and excrete the rest, becoming a wiser, clearer vessel than before. Both the courageous grandeur of the lion and the cowardly lion who runs from their own feelings, may be seen in someone who could benefit from Dandelion medicine. When we've done the processing, speaking up on issues comes from a more anchored place, rather than a reactive lashing out in anger.

The Spaces between, Hollow stem

Another theme in Dandelion is the importance of the spaces between - one of its seats of action. Whatever the space between, Dandelion helps to bring consciousness to these vulnerable places.

Whether it is the meeting place between the teeth and gums; the roots and soil; between humans and the Earth or any other in-between place that comes to mind, significant exchange and redistribution happens in these interactive spaces between the two.

The pause between thoughts and action, is a potent one. Allowing a pause before action allows important processing to occur before responding, which can make the difference between our expression coming from a place of liverish reaction or from an anchored, considered place. Dandelion and its seed clock encourages us to *take time.*

Dandelion can help take us into the in-between spaces when working with stuck patterns or addictions, so that we can pause and choose anew.

Cycles and circles.

Dandelion has weathered countless seasons and holds just as many teachings around time and cycles. Sit with a Dandelion plant to explore! From the qualities of patience, determination and longevity: *all in good time*; to sitting in the unknown spaces between: *only time will tell;* to displaying countless plant signatures around cycles, e.g. the flower blooms for one day - the solar cycle, the seed head appears to some as a moon, yet also speaks of the wisdom of oneness - many little seeds forming a beautiful sphere, each containing the wisdom of the whole plant to take with it as it spreads far, preparing to root and work its wisdom in a whole new cycle.

Dandelion in Summary

Dandelion Flower Code supports us to lower our centre of gravity, to connect deeply with our core and our roots and to get to the root of the matter.

It is particularly for when we are stuck, when the in-between spaces are blocked and not moving easefully. Grumpiness, ill humour, toxins in the body, liverishness and tension may all be apparent. When we are backed up with rubbish, when our places of exchange aren't functioning, we need Dandelion. When we aren't getting the messages, when our connections aren't working, look to Dandelion.

Dandelion supports us to clear from the centre outwards, to address the problem at its root rather than push it away and have it return endlessly via any number of addictions or avoidance mechanisms. Dandelion promotes us to be a clear vessel, a hollow stem. To have a healthy physical and emotional liver. It reminds us that when we are connected to our centre, there is no need to push or force things as our liver and our motions are in a state of easeful flow, processing as we go.

Dandelion used regularly over time is a champion to support the liver in this unloading and daily cleansing of both the physical and emotional.

Work with Dandelion flower code:
- If you are stuck or blocked.
- To help understand the root of stuck emotions, addictions or circular, repetitive patterns.
- To support healthy processing, so that you can release, let go and move forwards.
- As a general all-round support to detox, cleanse and process daily life.
- To enhance your capacity to become a clear vessel, *a hollow stem,* so your eternal self can be better expressed.
- To become more anchored in your core self.
- To remain grounded, centred and resilient in times of change.
- To learn more about cycles.

- To learn what it feels like to *rise rooted,* clear and anchored.
- Those who struggle to ground, or to stay anchored in self when interacting with others, or those who are too up in the head.
- Tension in body, especially upper areas - shoulders, neck. Liver issues. Use often over long periods.
- Anger issues. Reactivity. Grumpiness.

Yarrow - The Beauty of Embodiment

Achillea millefolium
Asteraceae

Yarrow

Herbal Introduction by Michelle Carnochan

The ancient peoples knew that the life of all flesh is in the blood, and I suspect that the 60,000-year-old Neanderthal human whose skeletal remains were also found with the remnants of yarrow between their teeth also knew this. As I sit at this time, in the womb cave of my moontime and feel the blood mysteries deep within my own bones, I am in the right place to contemplate Yarrow, a herb that interfaces between warrior and wise woman.

Linnaeus gave homage to the warrior archetype by giving Yarrow the Latin binomial *Achillea millefolium,* after Pliny the Elder's slightly embellished retelling of Homer's account (some 800 years prior) in *The Iliad* that Yarrow was the plant used by Achilles, who was taught by the centaur Chiron, to staunch the bleeding, alleviate the pain, and heal the wounds of his soldiers during the Trojan War. The late Australian herbalist Isabell Shipard even goes on to say that it was a bath of yarrow tea which Achilles was dipped in as his mother held on to his ill-fated heel. Nevertheless, it has been colloquially referred to by names such as Soldier's Woundwort, Knight's Milfoil, and Herba Militia ever since and has accompanied the army physicians of all sides on many a battlefield throughout the ages. (The name Yarrow itself is from an old Saxon word, but its meaning appears to be unknown). But Yarrow has been used all over the world in most long-lived traditional medicinal systems, and is also as at home in the midwife's kit, as it is in the army physician's, and she heals the wounds of the hidden battles that women also face.

I learned from herbalist Matthew Wood that Yarrow is known as the 'Master of the blood, working to the third level'. That is, it works with blood flow in the capillaries, veins *and* arteries as well as toning these vessels and stimulating the nerves responsible for opening and closing the arterioles in particular, according to need. And indeed, in thinking of arteries, the type of blood loss indicative of the need for Yarrow's help is typically fresh, bright red and fast flowing. It is blood full of life force. In my mind however, Yarrow is *Mistress* of the blood, being ascribed by Culpeper as a herb of Venus, stewarding this river of life, balancing its circulation and distribution, stopping the loss of vital fluid (and some might say our soul) and gathering us back into our body. She heals the separation that comes from trauma whether physical or spiritual.

Yarrow finds its place amongst the huge family of the Asteraceae. It is native to temperate regions of Europe, Asia and North America, but has accompanied people on their travels, often intentionally, and naturalised all over the world. It's feathery fern-like sword-shaped leaves, actually made up of many leaflets, give it it's second binomial *millefolium*, or 'thousand leaved', and it is commonly known by this name across Europe. The signature of the leaflets giving a deeply cut appearance implies it is for people who are cut to the bone – either literally or figuratively speaking. The white or sometimes pink or red flowers cluster in an umbel from a single stalk that grows between 30-60cm tall, whilst the leaves which can grow between 5cm-20cm long sheath the stem and form a rosette closer to the ground. Yarrow is a perennial that spreads over the ground by a creeping rhizome. It is said that the more stress the plant endures whilst growing, then the stronger its medicinal activity, and it is used in biodynamic farming as a compost activator to increase the micronutrient content of the soil, and as a companion plant which Rudolf Steiner said *"Yarrow is always the greatest boon...like sympathetic people in human society, who have favourable influence by their mere presence and not by anything they say."*

Energetically and relating to its virtues in the body, Yarrow is cooling and bitter, a stimulant and astringent. It is not only indicated for very bad wounds and the depletion that comes from excessive blood loss, but also for congestion of the blood with heat and swelling. Whilst being astringent and puckering and toning the tissue, Yarrow's action on diverting blood to the periphery and increasing circulation to the capillary bed, serves to both stop blood flow in a wound, as well as open the pores and induce sweating to relieve heat conditions such as fever and infection. In traditional European folk medicine, Yarrow has been used as both a treatment for the onset of flu and as a preventative in Winter in a hot tea along with the Elderflower and Peppermint.

For women, Yarrow regulates the menstrual cycle when there is excessive and heavy bleeding, or when the menses is scanty or absent. It is often used in combination with Shepherd's Purse to treat fibroids and is believed to reduce oestrogen excess (indicated by excessive bright red blood) and increase progesterone, making it also a very helpful ally for perimenopause. Austrian herbalist, Maria Treben recommended that all women from age 13-90 should take a cup of yarrow tea once per year to regulate the blood.

Its bitter taste stimulates digestive secretions, which in turn allows efficient movement in the gut. Along with previously mentioned properties, it is an effective ally for conditions such as Crohn's disease and ulcerative colitis. Yarrow is a mineral-rich herb, including cobalt which is necessary for the formation of intrinsic factor and vitamin B12 absorption and assimilation. Minerals such as calcium, magnesium, potassium, phosphorous and silica also no doubt contribute to its virtues including its pain-relieving properties. Yarrow also contains the vitamins A, B1, B2, Niacin and vitamin C.

When the summer-picked flowering tops of yarrow are distilled, it yields a beautiful cobalt blue essential oil. This includes constituents such as azulenes, cineol, camphor and thujone contributing to its anti-microbial properties. Other constituents include alkaloids, flavonoids, coumarins, tannins and saponins. The coumarins and salicylic acids may attribute to the virtue of being a blood thinner. In this regard, it is believed to absorb congealed blood after aneurism, stroke, brain or spinal injury, as well as in old bruises and blood blisters.

As much as Yarrow is associated with the legend of Achilles and being a heroic type of medicine, it also has a long history of magickal folklore associations. It has long been used for psychic protection and gathering in energies that have been depleted. In modern usage, Yarrow is also said to protect against or negate the effects of electromagnetic radiation. Yarrow is used in the Chinese divinatory system of the I Ching, and in European tradition its divinatory powers are employed to find one's true love. In the Hebrides, it was believed that one would attain the second sight by holding a leaf over one's eye.

Yarrow is best picked in the summer when in flower, but the leaves may be used as needed at any time. It can be used dried or fresh, made into tea, tincture or a vibrational essence. It is generally contraindicated during pregnancy (ed: when taken as a herb, but can be used in its homeopathic or flower code/essence form at this time). Yarrow is definitely a go-to for the first aid kit, and I personally would never be without her.

Yarrow Flower Code

Yarrow's core medicine is to support us to *integrate* and *embody* rather than avoid or suppress. Thus it contains both pictures. I find Yarrow a challenging herb to accurately express the plant spirit teachings of, because at every turn, the opposite is also true. That is a key to Yarrow! Paradox. The uniting of opposites and the integration of shadow parts that is so integral to wholeness or unified consciousness. While you'll see it subtly in most plants, in Yarrow it is a core theme.

So let's start with how Yarrow looks when it is a healthy complex within us. The yarrow deva described this via direct experience in my own body, embodiment being one of her main themes (think of Yarrow whenever you hear the new fad word 'somatic').

Embodiment

Yarrow speaks: *"Come home to your body. Feel what is there. Come back, call yourself back in. Stay focused and centred, don't drift off and out. Stand in your power. Contain it."*

Yarrow is a herb of embodiment. Deeply feminine, it teaches us to be present in our body and to feel *all* the pleasures and pains of being human. Its astringent action supports us to astringe ourselves fully into the physical body, so we can feel our boundaries and experience the life we are here to live. Yarrow helps us to fully process what's going on *through* our bodies, allowing emotions and experiences to integrate.

A healthy Yarrow state is to be deeply in the body. I can best describe it as the feeling of being a full cup, where all the senses are alive and switched on and there is a sense of deep connection and enjoyment WITHIN the body. All things are felt. The body is a delight to have. When we're in this state, release happens naturally - we stretch, yawn, sigh or sound as required. Nothing is suppressed or stored for later. Our body instantly deals with our world and experiences, moving them through us and integrating each moment. Think of an animal that yawns, twitches or naps as needed. All are different methods of processing information and experience. For anyone who isn't in this state, who doesn't feel the delight of having a body, Yarrow can be useful. Living in the disconnected, disembodied culture that we currently inhabit, virtually everyone could benefit from Yarrow's flower medicine.

The body needs sufficient time as well as rest in order to integrate and fully process all of our experiences. When we go through big events, more processing is required and we may need more time. Otherwise, the body starts to run on empty and survival mode may kick in. Tight, constricted, tense sensations can become apparent as the body attempts to hold onto its last resources. Injuries can be a common manifestation.

Yarrow is for being in the body. When we lose the containment of our body, we are on our way towards death. Excess bleeding and haemorrhages where our power starts leaking and literally bleeding out of the body is an external expression of when the containment and boundaries of our body have been breached or lost. Yarrow's astringency helps us *contain* our energy, to stay *in the body* and to process what has unfolded rather than drift off and out of ourselves. Yarrow stems bleeding. It keeps our life force in the body. Severe bleeding leads to a literal loss of consciousness, where we leave the body. This is the opposite to embodiment.

While Yarrow is known for protection, the best protection in the world is to be deeply embodied. The more in our bodies we are, the less we are shaken by external energies and the more able we are to stand firm in ourselves. Being in the body gives us a strong sense of our own boundaries. When we're disembodied or too open to external forces, we need Yarrow to bring us back in, to ground and feel our edges again. This is the way that Yarrow acts as protection.

Likewise, when going through periods of growth and evolution, Yarrow is a great support to help us integrate new learnings within our body. During big shifts, kundalini awakenings or rites of passage, this is so important as new states of awareness can leave us wide open to external harm before we have learnt to fully deal with the new realm we're experiencing. Remaining firmly within the bounds of your body allows any shifts to fully integrate, leaving you space to continue growing. Paradoxically, it is at times of the greatest embodiment (giving birth for example) that we travel into cosmic realms and have the capacity to stay embodied tested. To leave the body at this time, stops the evolutionary growth that this potent transformation can bring, and at its worst can lead to death. The more in our body we are, the further we can fly.

Yarrow supports integration time, it relaxes us so we can receive and allow our cup to fill up again.

Battle wounds.
The legend of Achilles receiving a fatal wound that could only be healed by using Yarrow *along* with a piece of the arrow that caused the wound has so much rich guidance within it. Yarrow as wound healer is the most obvious, but there is a deeper teaching of Yarrow within this story. That we must look to the source of the wound - the arrow - in order to heal. As we'll see, Yarrow encourages us to meet our wounds in order to grow through them, to face the inner battlefield of personal demons and to do the shadow work involved to become whole.

"The Pretty little herb of Venus."
Once known by this name, Yarrow is often considered to be a plant manifestation of the planet Venus and hence used to bring into balance all Venus qualities - the desire to connect, socialise, come together, unify and harmonise. This carries through to the physical body affecting the Venus organs such as the reproductive system.

On the opposite side of the coin is Mars - the battle warrior who desires to fight, divide and conquer. And it was fascinating learning from the Yarrow spirit that it contains Mars as a shadow energy. As such, it inherently contains the possibility and medicine of integrating these two aspects. Yarrow can bring the strength and fierce protective warrior energy that can stand up and fight for a cause, yet without the bloodshed of Mars. Yarrow heals the wounds of battle (of which childbirth was anciently included) as it is for haemorrhages and nasty wounds of all sorts.

Yarrow is a big remedy for female issues from menstrual and uterine problems, endometriosis, childbirth (postpartum haemorrhage especially) right through to menopause. It has an energetic similarity with prolactin chemistry - sometimes called the 'nesting hormone'. Nesting is the urge experienced by many pregnant women (and animals) to refurbish the house and *prepare the nest*. At the same time prolactin is also a protective hormone, bringing the energy of a lion that will rise up and fight if their young appears to be at risk. Prolactin increases vigilance as well as being responsible for lactation.

Yarrow is a feminine warrior.

Yarrow has the softest leaves that form a beautiful safe nest, yet the flower stalks are strong, upright and tall. Likewise, a mother with a thousand duties has this upright warrior strength, endurance and capacity to deal with the million chores of motherhood, yet at the same time remain soft with her child.

"Here we stand, hand in hand,
Feet on the earth for this time of rebirth.
United we stand, feet on the land,

We breathe as one, we will not be overcome."
Yarrow song

Connection and Union
It is through connection that Yarrow's strength and healing properties reside. Like Calendula, Yarrow tends wounds of separation, but from a different angle - with connection at its core. On the surface level, it can be seen in the bringing together of the lips of a wound to reunite tissue. But it likewise works on deep emotional wounds.

Whether it is disconnection from our lineage; from spirit; from sisters or brothers; the womb; our inner feminine; the earth; each other; cycles; our inner wisdom; from abundance (scarcity wounds) and so many more, Yarrow works with them all and helps reconnect us to pathways of receiving. Yarrow calls us to begin the process of reconnection and communication - whether it is between cells, tissues, people or different aspects of our psyche. It contains the teaching that unity and union is the only way to be whole.

"It is the web of connection that makes us strong. Our strength lies in our connectedness." How Yarrow plants grow with linked roots and in big bundles of many plants shows us a beautiful plant signature for these words from Yarrow.

Yarrow helps us to find the spark of sameness between all beings, to discover unity consciousness. In alchemy this is known as the *spirit* aspect, the vital force that is the same in all of us (where the *soul* is our uniqueness). When there are differences and wounds between two people, Yarrow can help us do the work involved within ourselves, so that we are then able to recognise our 'sameness' with the other (no matter how deeply hidden it may be).

While all plants ultimately lead to oneness, Yarrow is quite strong in reconnecting us to united fields and embracing diversity. Yarrow helps us to find the links between opposing sides, to find the common ground, the spirit within all. It is through finding the commonality and coming together via this, that strength and resilience arises. Yarrow is a strong survivor, it has been around for at least 40-60,000 years, and I suspect this is due to its ability to find the common force. Resilience and strength relies on an ability to find common ground with the world around us. The common spark of light within all beings. Working together and embracing differences creates a unified field that is a force to be reckoned with. Community consciousness.

Yarrow reconnects us with the unity of spirit, the oneness of all beings. The more we connect with this, the more layers of ego begin to fall away, and the more we appreciate the joy of having a body, and our unique part to play in the whole.

Shadow work. Integrating the opposites.
Because its quest is towards unity and reconnection, Yarrow is a herbal ally for shadow work - something that often stands in the way of wholeness.

Yarrow offers an invitation to have a deeper look at the shadow side within - all the parts that you have separated from. Generally, our shadow parts are projected onto the external world - that person who really annoys you, or the one you think is so amazing and you wish you were them - these are shadow aspects, parts we are so separate from we can't imagine having within us.

Working consciously with Yarrow, suppressed parts of ourselves may start to arise to be looked at, owned and integrated. Old traumas and battle scars included.

Yarrow itself, has a beautiful dual energy being both grounded and embodied with the steadfastness of a mountain that reaches high up into the cosmos to touch the stars. It integrates the heavens and earth.

It can help us to *integrate the opposites.* Masculine and feminine; heaven and earth; grounded embodiment and cosmic consciousness. When you work with Yarrow, you realise these supposed opposites are profoundly connected. That you can't reach to the stars without being deeply embodied and that our inner masculine and feminine exist simultaneously. That light and dark are intimately linked. That connection can't be known without knowing disconnection.

Yarrow work is to look to where we have polarised thinking and to learn to hold both and integrate two seemingly opposing forces in our being. The discover the ecstasy of paradox.

Yarrow invites us to find common ground. To integrate more of the world around us. Jung called this process *individuation* and his work has rich wisdom for those working with Yarrow. Shadow work is a call to unity consciousness. To begin the journey of embracing everything as an aspect of ourselves no matter how separate or different we feel from it. To embrace the opposites and find the place where they unite.

A very Yarrow example of this type of shadow work arose in the spagyric alchemy with Yarrow. We were taken to a time in ancient Egypt when beauty and beauty routines were being used by women as a way to control others, particularly men via *allurement.* Yarrow as the 'pretty little herb of Venus' started showing us its own shadow aspect - of using beauty and the web of connection for its own gain. There was a spidery energy of entrapment "come into my womb" apparent. This eventually helped lead to a fear of women and the patriarchy that came to pass. Yarrow showed us how women helped *create* male domination by misusing their own capacities.

So what stops us from being embodied and integrating learnings as we go? There are a few key pictures of Yarrow in here...

Survival mode, Trauma, Suppression.
For those who have been on the battlefield of life for long periods of time and are living in survival mode, there simply isn't the capacity to process big emotions or the traumas being lived. Natural disasters, war zones, refugees are at one end, but there are also the long labours of childbirth, or an ongoing situation of homelessness, or any other variety of situations where survival mode has been extensive, leading to trauma stored and suppressed for later. A picture of prolonged exhaustion is apparent. Wherever you just have to keep going even though you feel like collapsing, think Yarrow. Wherever emotions and traumas have been stored for later, think of Yarrow. It is a great support for those in long term survival mode, or those being stretched to the max, pushed to the very edges of their capacity. When we just have to keep going, sometimes the only way is to disconnect from the body.

Yet when we don't have the capacity or space to integrate our experiences and to process emotions so they can move through us, the body is impacted. Yarrow supports us to stay strong while gently allowing us to begin to integrate the situation through our bodies. It brings us gently back into the body if we have left it, reminding us of our boundaries. As a well-known remedy for colds, Yarrow works to strengthen our immune system, another boundary of protection.

Yarrow helps us to process, integrate and do the inner work that is required to be an embodied being evolving to wholeness.

Laziness, procrastinator, avoidant, suppressive.
On the other hand, there are those who don't do their inner integration and shadow work by choice!

Those in need of Yarrow are often adept at procrastination and avoidance techniques. They don't want to look at their shadow side or deal with their own shit. This is the negative avoidance culture we live in currently - a quick fix on social media to avoid feeling an emotion or addressing a problem. Yarrow is the kick up the ass remedy, to get you to put in the work that is required to face your shit rather than blame someone else, run from it or keep dodging it by focusing on the next endorphin hit. Another way avoidance can play out is through being incredibly busy and never stopping.

While these pictures are different to those in survival mode who literally don't have the capacity, the effect is similar - disconnection. Disconnection to self, to the body, to feelings and emotions.

Yarrow supports us to do the work, to face our suppressed feelings and shadow sides, to evolve into more whole versions

of ourselves. It brings us the strength to look within, the industriousness and the energy required to face our demons and come through the other side. It awakens the disciplined *warrior within* who is willing to face the inner battlefield with connection in order to evolve and grow. Yarrow is the great compost activator of biodynamic farming. It speeds up the composting process, literally helping to process the refuse and turn it into juice for the benefit of all. There is no difference to the healthy Yarrow person who does the same.

Yarrow in Summary
Yarrow as one of the healing herb codes, reminds us to be deeply in the body, for to know the sacred vessel of the body intimately and to feel everything of our earthly experience is "vital" (pun intended). Yarrow reminds us what a natural state of healthy embodiment feels like. It may look like a stretch, a yawn, a cry, a dance - allowing your body to move however it needs in order to express and integrate each experience. Yarrow reminds us that release is a natural process and that feelings are not meant to be stored or suppressed for later.

The more in our body we are, the more grounded we become, and this in turn helps us connect to the stars and to embody the lightness of spirit. In this way, Yarrow, through the process of grounded depth and embodiment, is a gateway to the stars. It helps us to integrate and embody life to the full and to stay in connection.

Work with Yarrow:
- The herbal somatic remedy. Trauma work. Brings strength, support and energy during deep shadow work, somatic work, processing trauma
- To integrate experiences/states, healed versions of self, and new ways of being.
- To develop healthy embodiment practices.
- Protection if the cause is not being fully present in the body. Those ever going out of body on spiritual quests but not integrating the work through the body.
- To develop the self-discipline and industriousness for inner work.
- To awaken the warrior within.
- Those in long term survival mode, to support the start to integrate and process, to return to body and gently release stored trauma.
- Disconnect of any sort - to bodies, feelings, emotions.
- To understand unity consciousness.
- Grounding and cosmic at the same time.
- To integrate the paradox of opposing forces.
- For procrastinators, avoidance adepts, laziness. Or too busy and industrious to look within. On the run from shadow work.
- For those who are stretching themselves on all levels - evolving to the max, pushing their limits and boundaries, going beyond constantly.

Chamomile - Inner child

Matricaria chamomilla
Asteraceae.

Chamomile

Herbal Introduction by Pam Scott

Chamomilla comes from the Greek 'chamos' meaning 'ground' and 'melos' meaning 'apple.' Originally native to parts of Europe and Asia, it is now popular and cultivated all over the world. There are two types of chamomiles used in herbal medicine, which can be used interchangeably, though the German is considered to have the more potent medicinal action. They are both sown in spring and prefer a sunny position in a well-drained soil. Harvest flowers from both species in the morning when the flowers are fully open. Pinch the flowers just beneath their heads and leave the stems intact to encourage new flowers. The flowers should dry in a couple of weeks and then store in a cool dark place. They can also be frozen.

German Chamomile (*Matricaria chamomilla*) is a self-seeding annual that can grow up to about 30cm high. It has a smooth feathery stem with many flowers that have a hollow conical centre and is considered to be more medicinal than the Roman Chamomile flowers. *Matricaria* comes from 'mater' meaning 'mother' and 'cara' meaning 'beloved'. In Latin 'matrix' means 'womb'.

In German it is *Kamillenbluten* which means 'capable of anything' as it has a positive effect on many organs in the body and is claimed to heal sickly plants growing nearby.

Roman Chamomile (*Anthemis Nobilis*) is also known as Ground Apple due to its apple-like scent, as well as Barnyard Daisy or Lawn Chamomile. It is a perennial plant that is well established in a few months and easily propagated with division. Low growing, with a single flower on a hairy stem that has a solid flat centre, it is more fragrant than German Chamomile although not necessarily more medicinal. If a person has a sensitivity to plants in the Asteraceae family, an allergic response is more likely with the Roman Chamomile.

Both Chamomiles contain terpenoids, volatile oils, flavonoids, polyphenols, coumarins, polysaccharides, aromatic, mucilage, sesquiterpenes, and their actions are nervine, sedative, anti-inflammatory, antihistamine, antispasmodic, vulnerary, antimicrobial, antifungal, diaphoretic and emmenagogue.

There has been much written about the cure-all effects of Chamomile by many cultures throughout history and it was so important that it was said that one should always bow their head to a Chamomile plant.

Ancient Egyptians considered it to be a cure-all for all ailments and was used in their embalming process. It was considered so significant that they dedicated it to their sun god Ra. The beneficial effects were also noted by the Anglo Saxons who included it as part of their sacred herbs when praying for the sick. This belief in the herb was also carried through to people's houses. It was hung in windows and doorways to ward off evil and insects as well as to attract good fortune. As a good fortune charm, it had the ability to make you more attractive to others and to attract luck, especially if you washed your hands or bathed in it.

Hippocrates, Dioscorides and Galen wrote of its medicinal benefits, unlike Culpeper who considered it to be so popularly known that he wrote very little about it.

Asclepiades thought Chamomile to be the first remedy of choice before all others.

Primarily known for its soothing, calming and anti-inflammatory benefits, it has far-reaching effects throughout the body via its beneficial relationship to the vagus nerve. This 10th cranial nerve is the longest nerve of the autonomic nervous system, which involves both the fight, flight or freeze response of the sympathetic nervous system; and the rest and digest state of the parasympathetic nervous system. The vagus is a large nerve that begins in the brain and carries on through the heart, eyes, ears, nose, mouth, skin, respiratory and digestive areas, and right into the abdominal and pelvic cavity. It is involved with all of the voluntary and involuntary functions in the body that we take for granted. Many stresses or dis-eases will impact on one or all of these body functions at some stage.

Chamomile is at its best wherever there is heat and tension. It soothes allergic reactions of all types. It may present as an allergic reaction on the skin and appear as a rash. A poultice may help earaches, toothaches and puffy or inflamed eyes. The one recommendation that Culpeper *did* write about was to boil the Chamomile flowers in lye for a healthy scalp. It makes a great scalp tonic for dandruff and a chamomile hair rinse brightens blonde hair.

It has been considered a mother's herb and early Christians dedicated it to the Virgin mother. It has been helpful for menstrual problems including pain, or any condition associated with the womb.

It is for babies of any age who are irritable and willful. With the younger Chamomile types, it takes out the heat and pain of nappy rash, teething problems (one red cheek specifically), growing pains and colic. It can reduce allergic reactions, tension and inflammation in the gastrointestinal tract. We know Peter Rabbit's mother sent him to bed with a cup of Chamomile to settle his stomach after he came home upset from being chased by Mr. McGregor. It is beneficial for so many digestive issues. There may be many emotions held in here.

It is helpful for people who relive their past experiences over and over again as they seek a way to process it. They may get stuck in the story and feel unable to move on. There can be a feeling of having been abandoned by something or someone but really it is they who have abandoned themselves. They may have been searching for nurturing and nourishment outside of themselves and for something that no one else can fulfill. Maybe with Chamomile, they can appreciate that all they look for externally is within and it can aid in digesting these experiences and enable them to move forward.

Contraindications: Those who have allergic responses to plants in the Asteraceae family may have a reaction to Chamomile. Roman Chamomile is thought to be the most likely culprit. Traditionally considered a child/pregnancy herb, it is currently not recommended in pregnancy as there have been instances where it was thought to stimulate contractions or create circulation issues with the baby. Drinking the tea in moderation is suggested.

(Note: the flower code essences have no contraindications so can be used at any time as they are energetic essences.)

Chamomile, as one of the healing herb codes is helpful for remembering and restoring a state of *Deep Inner Trust.* In the body, this manifests as a calm, relaxed, healthy nervous system and a connection to our centre. Able to easily digest all that occurs in the external world, this core centredness and inner trust allows us to maintain the innocence of a child at play, whose inner light radiates out into the world. Chamomile is a plant that can activate our inner light and reconnect us with the source of power that resides within us.

Summer Solstice
Chamomile energetically is a little akin to the Summer solstice. The summer solstice is a moment of fullness at the peak of the year, when the external boundaries are reached and the solar light of the day is at its longest. It is also the point at which energies begin their spiral journey inwards again, when the days will ever so slowly become shorter on the path towards winter. Late pregnancy is an example of this phase of full ripeness in a woman - where the slow spiralling inward to a place of deep body wisdom and inner trust begins, which will eventually culminate in birth.

Chamomile likewise brings us in from the periphery and back to centre. A Chamomile abdominal compress gives a full experience of this. By being firmly wrapped like a swaddled babe, an awareness of our edges and boundaries and a calling back to the centre of our being - the solar plexus - is encouraged. Many people describe the experience as *a big warm hug.* In effect, it is an embodied version of the ancient Summer Solstice ritual in which the villagers would walk the perimeter of town to reinstate the village boundaries, reaffirming its protection for the year ahead.

Chamomile is also an important skin remedy - our skin being a personal boundary, the meeting point of outer and inner. Chamomile yields a beautiful blue essential oil, a signature for its ability to cool, soothe and bring us inwards again, to balance the peak fire of the summer season with the watery inwardness that it contains. It is a beautiful herb for bringing calm at peak times, like summer when the days are long, the sun is hot and the energy is outward and often hectic and we can easily get *fried* both literally by the sun, and within the nervous system.

Deep inner trust

Healthy Chamomile is a state of *Deep Inner Trust.* When we have trust deep within then we relax. Centred to the core, we can be present to the goings on of the external realms without being spun out of balance by them. Much like a buddha, we can stay still at the centre of the eternal spinning wheel of life.

An absence or loss of deep inner trust and connection to our source can manifest in many ways. Abandonment issues, an overwhelmed nervous system, attempts to control the external world from the arising fear that accompanies loss of connection with our centre, are common manifestations. Controlling the world around us, even our own breathing are compensatory ways that aim to give us a (false) sense of power amidst the chaos. Chamomile can slowly return us to our core, to trust in ourselves and all that is.

Core centre. Solar Plexus.

At the core of our being is the belly, the solar plexus. This is the place where the umbilical cord to source once lay. In utero it connected us to the placenta and mother who fulfilled all of our energy requirements in the womb. After birth, this core connection is no longer necessary, the cord gradually dries up and drops away as our source requirements change. Though when the cord is severed too early (still a common hospital practice), a sense of abandonment and a chamomile presentation may result and persist well into adult life.

The solar plexus is like our personal sun. When this solar centre is inhabited in a healthy way, relaxed and calm, we digest experiences and food with ease. All sorts of digestive complaints can occur when we abandon our solar centre. Anxiety, stress, emotional tension and a myriad of complaints all stem from this loss of connection or faith in the power that resides within us.

Chamomile acts to return us to our centre, our inner source, the light within. It soothes and calms the belly, calling us back there, bringing us deeper into the rest and digest state of a relaxed nervous system. It helps us release emotional tension held in the gut.

Chamomile helps us to inhabit our gut, to trust our gut feelings, to know when 'something is not right.' If we are not listening to this inner knowing, we effectively abandon ourselves - looking outwards rather than inwards for answers.

If we have become focused on the periphery instead of within our centre, then Chamomile can help us return. It may be that we easily get caught up and distracted by external stimuli, which can manifest in over-sensitivities of all types, including many allergies for which Chamomile is well known for.

Nervous System

Chamomile helps us process and 'digest' emotions in order to unwind, relax and sleep. When we are centred, we can process all external stimuli calmly and with ease. The periphery is not the focus. We can return to the image of the buddha who remains in inner stillness despite external chaos. The buddha is generally depicted with a lovely fat belly too - he is inhabiting his gut, completely *in the body.* A healthy Chamomile.

Those in need of Chamomile's sweet teachings are those who have lost their centre and are overly focused on the periphery and the external realm. This often leads to an overloaded nervous system as the central processing is not fully engaged.

Several physical themes in Chamomile are common manifestations of this:
- digestive complaints - if we abandon the solar plexus or are not listening to the gut, then the gut may cry out for attention.
- oversensitivity/allergies - an inability to process as the system is overloaded, 'fried' and reactive;
- skin irritations such as eczema, rashes, irritations. The skin is our physical periphery and may be the last resort if we are not processing through our centre.
- When we are not in our core power, we are also much more open to external influences and disease. (Chamomile was one of the nine sacred herbs of the

Anglo Saxons used to ward off disease. The tea on the skin is used as an insect repellent, and in the garden to discourage infestation. It was thrown over thresholds to keep evil spirits away.)

In homeopathy, Chamomilla is hypersensitive to pain out of all proportion to the *actual* pain. These people are on edge, the slightest thing feels enormous, their nervous system can't take any more. They are unable to cope, completely overloaded and unable to process.

Chamomile soothes and calms the nervous system and contains the potent medicine of being able to stay calm even amongst hectic busy energy.

The leaves of Chamomile have a lovely plant signature being reminiscent of a fat, relaxed nervous system. Returning to the healthy Chamomile image as a woman in the late phases of pregnancy (in a healthy expression) - her nerves are relaxed, there is a sense of fullness coupled with the purity and innocence of carrying the light of a child within. She carries a deep inner trust in her body, has a heightened awareness and radiates oxytocic beauty from the new life she carries. Both pregnancy and breastfeeding are dominated by a state of being *in the body*. Being centred in the belly rather than the head. This is a positive Chamomile state, which Chamomile can help us return to if we are not fully there. (You'll notice the overlaps with yarrow and a slight similarity in their leaf structure too).

Abandonment

When we have moved out to the periphery of our lives, we are in essence, abandoning our core self. When we are not listening and following our deeper truth - that quiet little voice that waits patiently in the background to be heard - we abandon ourselves. No matter what is going on in the external realm, deep within there is always a state of peace that can be found behind it all. However, as a culture, we are more often distracted by the loud peripheral voices of the ego and external irritations rather than staying centred in ourselves.

Abandonment of self can be very subtle. It can be doing so much there is no time to refill your cup. It can be so much busy-ness rushing around doing, that you forget what your core focus originally was. It can be not having enough stillness in your life in order to actually know what you really want or to make decisions from your centre. It can be placing your trust and authority outside yourself or an excessive focus on what others think, recommend or say. It can be not knowing what your gut instincts or womb are telling you.

At your core, the place of deep inner trust and peace, your true self knows what you really want and need. But it may require a peaceful, calm, relaxed, centred state to hear it. Working with the Chamomile deva can help on both accounts.

Often it is easier to focus on external energies (other people, situations, objects) and make them our power source. We may fear our own power and the responsibility it brings. But when we place our source outside of ourselves, our deepest self feels abandoned, unheard, sad, angry and irritated. Our solar plexus chakra suffers and we may suffer digestive or solar plexus complaints. But most of all we are not letting our own light and our power shine.

Focusing on the needs of others excessively can be one of the craftiest ways we hide our light behind a bushel. Under the cover of helping others, we abandon ourselves. When fulfilling the needs of others becomes our only power source, our solar plexus and inner self can feel a deep sense of abandonment and complain bitterly. Alternatively, when you shine your light from a healthy place, guided by your core, everyone around you will benefit from the glow that emanates.

Looking for acknowledgement from others or the external world can be another subtle form of abandoning our core knowing. Whether it is doing what others recommend or say without tuning in to feel if we resonate with it; whether it is waiting for external confirmation even when you *know* what is right for you, but not following through until someone agrees; or whether it is simply always looking outside for the answers – all of them are a form of handing your power over, of subtle lack of faith in your inner knowing, of abandonment of your core self. This is the realm of Chamomile.

Inner Child and Mother

It is no wonder we live in a culture so in need of Chamomile, with our power constantly placed externally and not based deep within ourselves. Much of this goes back to the very early years - early cord clamping, mother child bonding interruptions, birth, postnatal and parenting practices that interrupt rather than support natural processes, controlled feeding/sleeping/crying, the list continues throughout childhood. Wherever our inner knowing was transgressed, unheard or forfeited for external knowledge (that went against our inner body wisdom), we have undergone an abandonment to our core self. Wherever our inner child experienced (whether real or imagined) an abandonment in this way, a little bit of trust is chipped away within.

Chamomile can show us where we're at with our own inner bonding. Chamomile work is akin to inner child work. Recalling *matricaria* pertains to *matrix* - the womb (the physical inner mother), there is a lot to be said about learning to parent ourselves in healthy ways and to be able to listen to the inner child within us and its needs. The inner child holds the authentic, innocent self within it. Developing healthy bonds with our inner child by listening to its needs, parenting as needed, playing, and also bringing in healthy boundaries (skin), our capacity to *trust* again builds. Chamomile is a physical, emotional and spiritual support to this process. It will show you where this needs attention in your life.

Chamomile has a very clear picture in homeopathy - grumpy, rude, irritable, pretend they don't want attention when they really do. They ask for something, but when it's given they don't want it anymore. They simply can't be pleased. There is a state of disarray. Nothing satisfies. It shows up often around teething times, they have one red cheek. They can't deal with pain. They are having a painful experience, a prime time for the outer parent to hold them in this difficulty, to simply 'be with'. This teaches the child how to 'be with' and embrace life in all its facets. To learn a healthy model that can be used for inner parenting throughout life. If we didn't experience this, we need more than ever to develop it for ourselves as adults. To parent the inner tantrumming child, to be with it.

Light activation

Chamomile activates our inner light the same way the sun activates photosynthesis in plants. Soothing the nervous system and slowing us down in order to metabolise effectively, Chamomile guides us to find our inner source of power, our inner light and to let it shine. It helps us remember that everything we need to shine is within us, and that when we are searching externally for power, we are effectively handing our power over.

Chamomile is sensitive to light and can help us recognise all the ways we avoid owning our light and power, where we fear our own power and block it, or where we believe that light is *outside* of us and is something we need to 'get' externally.

Light activates our DNA, awakening our true selves. Every cell within us contains a spark of light, and our solar plexus plays a role as a centre of this inner light. Remembering and activating our inner light is to empower ourselves and rediscover that the true source of our power lies within.

Chamomile was sometimes known as the Plant Doctor for its capacity to heal any unwell plant that grows nearby. Healthy connection with our core self, our inner knowing and our own power can heal virtually anything.

The Camomile shall teach thee patience
Which riseth best when trodden most upon.
The More the Merrier 1608. Shakespeare.

Chamomile in Summary

Chamomile has learned how to find the calm place no matter what, so it can help us to do that too. For those who are oversensitive or hypersensitive to pain, whose nervous systems are on high alert, it can help find peace and encourage our shining sun to keep beaming out.

Chamomile can find light in the hardest of times. It can take you back to the deep peace behind the irritation, the light that is always there even when the clouds appear to be blocking it.

When we are hypersensitive, when there's too much going on, and we just can't process it all, if we get allergies, anger, or an overactive nervous system that needs soothing and calming, Chamomile is there like a soothing mother to hold. Chamomile is at its prime when the energies are hectic and outward like summer solstice - if we are unable to process it all, it can feel very tiring. Chamomile brings us back to the belly, to the rest and digest phase to support us.

Work with Chamomile:
- To find deep inner trust in yourself. When you've lost faith in self.
- To develop the capacity to listen to your gut and knowing.
- To heal and feel the first abandonments and hurts of life. The ones where we lost our innocence and naive trust in the world (overlaps with English Daisy).
- Inner child work. Building our capacity to bond our adult and child selves in a healthy manner.

- To explore healthy bonding patterns - which come from being centred in our own core/self.
- Abandonment issues - from others, but also from not listening to your inner self.
- Giving power to others. Following guidance from purely outside sources. Naivety and faith in others without listening to self.
- Controlling patterns. Based in fear rather than trust.
- To calm, soothe and support the processing and digesting of life. (Yarrow overlap)
- To return to centre if you've been pulled too far out. Core issues. To return to your inner source. When your attention is over-external and lost capacity to feel inner core and knowing.
- Grumpy, irritable, hypersensitive, nothing satisfies.
- To find your inner light and let it shine.
- To find the real source of your power within.

Rosemary – Divine Feminine

Rosmarinus officinalis/Salvia Rosmarinus
Lamiaceae

Rosemary

Herbal Introduction by Michelle Carnochan

Over the course of my life, I have often had opportunity to reside in the presence of a Rosemary guarding the threshold of the house. Presently, there is a large Rosemary shrub in my peripheral vision that is commanding me to write of her. And she does have a commanding presence. Her delicate pale blue blossoms speak of gentleness, but really belie the powerful healing that she offers.

I can't help but be reminded of the aroma of a Sunday roast and see the ritual gathering of family when I smell or taste Rosemary's rich pungency. I crush a resinous sprig between my fingers and inhale deeply. The scent penetrates and infuses my core. Its warmth diffuses strength into my heart and comfort to my soul. A richness, that recalls images of tapestries interwoven with fine threads of gold, which shimmer and dance in the firelight of the hearth, speaking the stories of previous generations. Rosemary is a herb of the hearth, and the hearth belongs to a queen. This queen isn't afraid to cut through the fat, to expose the bare bones of truth and to seek the nourishing marrow within to feed her people.

There's an old folk saying "where Rosemary flourishes, the lady rules." In my mind, this speaks to the nurturing and protection of the Divine Mother that Rosemary invokes.

This particular Rosemary shrub that is speaking to me invokes Boudicca, that ancient Celtic warrior queen who stood against the patriarchal Romans to protect her daughters, her home, her hearth, and the culture of her people. Another Rosemary may invoke the Queen of Hungary for instance, famed for the aromatic water named after her 'for outward application to renovate the vitality of paralysed limbs' (Mrs M. Grieve. 'A Modern Herbal'). In France, she is associated with Mother Mary.

Gentle, nurturing, and fierce protectress, this is a herb that kindles the inner fire. In this archetype, we often see the element of self-sacrifice. I see Rosemary for those who give much of themselves but have depleted all reserves. It is one of the quintessential Mother herbs, reminding the nurturers to also hold the space and nurture themselves.

"Rosemary, that's for remembrance. Pray you, love, remember." Ophelia (Hamlet by William Shakespeare).

Rosemary has a very long and ancient history of use throughout the Mediterranean region and wherever the Romans and other wayfarers took her, and she has a long association with the memory. Ancient Greek, and English Elizabethan-era students wore Rosemary wreaths to help retain what they were studying. It was also worn at weddings and funerals to symbolise loyalty and friendship - both acts of keeping loved ones at the forefront of our minds.

16th century herbalist, John Parkinson said of Rosemary "it helpeth also a weak memory by heating and drying up the cold moistures of the braines, and quickening the senses." As such, his successor and famed herbalist Culpepper placed it under the dominion of the Sun, and further extolled its virtues as a warming herb, which includes 'lifting the spirits' and 'dispelling the mood', an encouraging anti-depressant. Yet for her feminine energies and work on healing the red thread of the ancestral womb as well as regulating the menstrual cycle, we might also consider her a herb of Venus.

It is via its action on the digestion, and in particular on the gallbladder that we see this virtue of 'cutting through the fat' not just metaphorically, but quite literally. Rosemary helps the liver and the gallbladder to deal with rich dietary excesses by stimulating the flow of bile. And as an antioxidant, she simulates glutathione production and thus helps not only to protect the liver but also the blood vessels, heart, nerves, and brain.

Rosemary also has an anti-inflammatory action; is antispasmodic and can be used in the prevention of asthma or to treat a cold and moist spasmodic cough; has anti-tumour properties; can be used for under-active thyroid; and is a powerful preventative for Alzheimer's.

She both stimulates circulation throughout the body, stimulates the nervous system, is relaxant and calming, and tones the digestion. This polarity can be applied both internally and externally. We might work with her in an infused oil or liniment for muscular tension and soreness, or for stimulating the scalp in hair loss. Internally, I might consider her a whole-body tonic, for typically cold and weak people (or those prone to debilitation from chronic stress, for example) with fogginess and/or poor memory, prone to bouts of depression and/or anxiety, and poor digestion of fats in particular, where gas and bloating are present as well as general inflammation of the gut. Rosemary is not one that I would give to a hot, angry, hypertensive sort of person. But for someone who has lost heart. For someone who feels stuck in body or mind. Or someone who needs their inner flame reignited.

From her first classification by Linnaeus up until 2017, Rosemary went by the Latin binomial *Rosmarinus officinalis*, meaning 'dew of the sea.' This beautiful moniker honoured both her native habitat, growing around the Mediterranean on dry, stony, and calcareous soil, often on cliffs or hill sides where she is watered by the sea mists. In 2017 the classification was changed to *Salvia rosmarinus*, and whilst this upset many a herbalist, not only causing confusion and a recalibration of once universal scientific nomenclature, it also invoked a feeling that the Divine Mother once again was being usurped by a patriarchal urge to be the saviour (which is the meaning of the Latin *Salvia*). Perhaps however, we might view this change as reflecting the healing properties of restoring remembrance of the Divine Feminine in the collective consciousness?

Rosemary's growth habits speak of an inner strength and resilience. She often faces high winds and is a pioneer plant of degraded soils. In cultivation, she requires a sunny spot and although she likes well-drained soil, Rosemary also thrives in sandy, poor soil. She can handle the heat well and is drought tolerant.

A member of the Lamiaceae (mint) family, she is strongly aromatic. You can feel these aromatic oils as much as you can smell them, by the resinous quality of its short, sharp, narrow leaf. The leaves grow opposite to each other on slender upright woody stems. Its small white or pale blue flowers appearing in pairs at the end.

Rosemary's active principles include essential oils (cineole, pinene, camphor, borneol, limonene, terpineol and verbinol), phenolic acids (rosmarinic), bitter triterpenes (carnosol, rosmanol), triterpenes (oleanic and frolic acid), triterpene alcohols, flavonoids and their glycosides (diosmetin, luteolin).

A key indication for working with Rosemary is when one seeks *to warm and strengthen, to get things moving and to help things flow, to protect.* This can be applied physically, emotionally, mentally, spiritually, and magickly.

The leaves can be gathered at any time of the year, but Rosemary is at her peak when she is flowering. Gather the flowering tops and hang in a warm dry place in bunches to dry. Once dried, strip the leaves from the stem and store in an airtight container in a cool, dark, dry place. They can then be used to make an infused oil, tea, or a tincture. She can also be used freshly picked in these applications.

Often, I just like to have a sprig of fresh rosemary sitting next to me as I study or work, which I can pick up and smell when I need to remember something important. But most of all, I find her presence comforting.

Rosemary Flower Code

Rosemary, the *dew of the sea* (ros marinus). While *mar* or *mer* refers to the ocean, it is also the root of *mother* (e.g. *la mere* in French). The two are fractals of each other, ocean and mother - the feminine principle itself. Rosemary is akin to the distilled drops of the ocean – a distillation of *mother*. In English it has interestingly become *Rose Mary*. Mary's Rose. The love of the mother is like an ocean after all, never-ending and expansive.

Rosemary is one of the great healing herb flower codes that helps us to find our way back to embodying the divine mother within.

Water, grief, tears and ocean.
One of the legends of Rosemary is of Mother Mary and Mary Magdalene escaping the Middle East after the crucifixion. Landing on the coast of southern France at a place that is now named Saintes Maries de la Mer (St. Mary of the sea), Mother Mary was fatigued from fleeing and rested under a Rosemary bush. On leaving, she left her blue cloak (some say it was the same cloth used to swaddle Jesus) on the Rosemary bush, and this is how the flowers came to be sky blue. When listening to the Rosemary deva one day, she expanded this story more to me. Mother Mary in her pale blue robe was energetically releasing tears of grief at the loss of her home, her child and her past. Her tears appeared to me as the colour of Rosemary flowers with the feeling of an ocean of grief, that flowed back to the sea. The image contained a clue to the flower code and the medicine she holds. Salty tears are akin to the 'dew of the sea' and Rosemary carries the distillation and wisdom that comes from feeling deeply, grieving and releasing.

Rosemary grows on the salty windswept coast where sailors at sea were known to smell its scent long before land was sighted, reminding them of home and helping to guide them back to the hearth. Even its flavour has a touch of saltiness.

Part of Rosemary's teaching is the power of release and letting go through our tears. A process which provides a beautiful cleansing. Grief unexpressed can become like a cloud in the head, and just as a cloud releases raindrops, when we release our tears, the head grows clear again. Rosemary is a vast support for those experiencing grief or loss. It helps to relax and allow the emotions to move through us, to not hold back in the fear that the ocean is too big, but to surrender into our feelings and let them flow as they arise. It is through the shedding of our salty tears that we can eventually come back to our senses and remember not just ourselves, but all the blessings of whatever we have lost. Rosemary helps us dive into the ocean of emotion, while at the same time bringing a touch of fire to prevent us from drowning.

Rosemary is very connected to the phase of passing over, of death and ancestors, of remembering those who have passed and of honouring our ancestors. Elementally, it relates to the crossing over from the earth realm into the watery realms of the collective, the release of the body into unity again, yet somehow it helps us to make this crossing and still retain our unique spark of light. It may not so much be for the one crossing over the life death threshold, but for the ones left behind to help them 'stay alive' in a sense, though this could be extended to protect the soul as it navigates the watery realms of the underworld. After all, Rosemary has long been used at funerals, in ancient Egyptian tombs and more recently Remembrance Day. But more than that it was used as protection when around those dying, from pestilence, disease, evil spirits and witchcraft. It could be thought of for those who are around these thresholds of death and life (caregivers, death doulas, final days of a loved one, are a few examples), to protect their own spark of light and vitality from being pulled into the collective watery underworlds of those who have passed.

Rosemary is a great support for those who are lost in grief, and especially for the loss of a child. Rosemary helps us grieve fully. To not avoid the feelings that arise, but to dive deeply into our grief. In this way, we eventually come back to ourselves, our senses and the present moment, with a clearer brain and a strong loving memory. Until the next wave arises. She brings gentle fire to break through the clouds of grief, stimulating our minds back to clarity.

Rosemary is filled with love and empathy and supports us deeply in these times of our lives - to surf the fluctuating tides of emotion as they rise and fall, offering strong support to remember ourselves after the dissolution process of grief. To put ourselves back together again. To re-member.

Divine Feminine/Divine Mother

Just as Calendula needs to have a dose of the feminine in order to be a healed version of the masculine, Rosemary shows us how the healed or divine feminine needs a dose of the masculine integrated within. If we're drowning in a sea of emotion, we need a touch of fire to stimulate us. If we're losing ourselves in the collective ocean, we need a little dose of ego or 'self-ness' to remember ourselves. Rosemary contains this beautiful blend of yin and yang. It contains the warmth and stimulation required to keep a watery world balanced.

Rosemary holds the archetype of the *divine mother*. She helps us to get in touch with the divine mother within ourselves and thus to lovingly tend and heal any areas where this archetype is wounded or out of balance. She supports us to remember the way of the mother, the ocean. This extends to the physical body and the physical organ of the inner mother - the womb.

The divine mother archetype has a deep capacity to feel and to allow and hold space for all feelings and emotions. She is able to surrender to them and allow them to wash through her without holding on. She is a vessel for the ever-flowing currents.

Rosemary can awaken within us our capacity to mother ourselves, to hold space for our feelings so that they can be released. A healthy Rosemary knows how to nourish, nurture and mother not just others, but *ourselves*.

When we avoid experiencing our emotions or listening to our feelings, they cannot pass through us and become stuck. They literally are *held* in the body. In Rosemary this can show up as tired, tense muscles anywhere – often seen in the jaw, neck or shoulders. The amount of energy required to hold onto these feelings is exhausting and literally causes pain and muscular tension. Rosemary is for when we're holding on. It may be because we fear forgetting what we resist releasing, but the impact of this can throw us off balance. A healthy memory comes from moving through the emotions so we can be present to the now.

Mother love and wounds
Rosemary is a teacher and plant embodiment of the divine mother and tuning into her, it is hard not to feel a beautiful, all-encompassing love and sense of place or home. As divine mother, she shares how the role of 'mother' is to be a vessel for something far greater than herself, while at the same time not becoming attached to the role itself. While she gives it her everything, it is not her everything.

In her motherly love, she releases her own attachments, knowing that her child needs to grow and knowing when it's time to let go, even if it's sad. And as she does, she feels her grief and lets it flow, which allows the release process to unfold and the present to evolve. This is the *divine mother.*

Because human mothers will very rarely be divine mother energy all of the time, Rosemary is one of those herbs that virtually everyone can benefit from at some time or another, to help to remember the higher aspects of this divine feminine energy within ourselves.

Anywhere that is out of balance in the realm of *mother* can arise when working with Rosemary and we'll cover a few of the common presentations that this beautiful herb teaches of.

For those who have never experienced divine mother energy for whatever reason, think of Rosemary. Maybe the mother (or inner feminine aspect in parenting) was absent in some way. For all issues with mother or mother wounds, think of Rosemary. Not only does it help us to grieve the loss of this aspect in our early lives, but Rosemary can help us discover the divine mother energy *within* ourselves and awaken it in our being.

Motherhood entails a constant series of releasing as, one tiny step after the other, our child slowly separates and gains its independence. Commencing at birth and continuing at least until they have become fully independent. Each of these growths requires a little more letting go from the mother, and may involve a grieving process. While it's a natural and healthy part of mothering, it doesn't mean it won't feel sad sometimes. If there are emotions to be felt, they need to be felt. Rosemary helps us to really embody the release process rather than try to hold on when our child is ready to evolve. Mother love at its core.

Rosemary flower code helps beautifully when this independence is not fostered or where there is an unhealthy level of mothering or co-dependency between mother and child for whatever reason. Sometimes it is an overidentification with the mother role itself that pushes the relationship out of balance. Or it may be that we love being needed by our child, that it fulfils us in a way that may have been lacking in our own childhood journey. The mechanisms that play out from wanting to hold on to our child needing us for longer, can be very subtle, yet the result is the same and prevents the evolution of our child to a more independent, self-sufficient being at whatever stage or age of life. I've seen Rosemary flower code work wonders in these sometimes very subtle, imbalances in the mother child relationship. Wherever there is co-dependency between mother and child that is not in balance for their age, look to Rosemary.

Rosemary supports mothers to do the release work and grieve the little losses as their child grows. It is also for mothers who literally lose a child in some way and the deep grief that this evokes. It will not make the grieving process any less, but it will support and help to find moments of sunshine and happy memories amidst the tears.

At a deeper level, Rosemary helps us to find our inner mother. It may show up all the places and ways that we are not nurturing or nourishing ourselves. It may be where we are holding onto emotions rather than feeling them. Many women find the divine feminine aspect in themselves when they become a literal mother and a source of nurturing and nourishment for a child. However, the healthy inner mother is also able to nourish and care for the self. If we are only able to do this for others but not for ourselves, then we have some Rosemary healing to do.

As a summary, Rosemary is useful for all mother wounds whether you are in the child or mother role. For the deep griefs and losses - of losing a child, or the constant losses of a child growing up, for empty nest syndrome when the child leaves home and we realise we've somehow forgotten who we are beyond the mother role. These are times to invite Rosemary into our lives. It can help us experience and learn about the energy of divine mother if we have never had that modelled to us or tapped into it within as well as help us learn how to mother ourselves.

Rosemary holds the coding for how to be a divine mother - a vessel for creation with a deep role as nurturer while still maintaining a sense of self and appropriate self-care. She is not overidentified with the mother role, yet fulfils it with grace and love. She has unconditional love for all beings, not just her own offspring. While she will always protect her child and give it the personal love it requires, it is *never* at the expense of another.

Womb work

The mother within our physical body is the womb. The womb is our physical sacred vessel of creation, which provides the space, the nourishing soil *and* the ocean that feeds our seeds and brings them into being. It is part of the womb's role to hold us.

Any sort of womb work is mother/Rosemary work. The inner mother and hence Rosemary, relates to our capacity to nourish and hold ourselves in unconditional love. The part of us that can hold and soothe and love no matter what is going on, like a mother that soothes a crying babe with her soft touch, voice and presence.

Rosemary relates to our capacity to hold ourselves and feel the feels. It has the beautiful effect of relaxing voluntary muscles (the action/external muscles), while toning and gently stimulating the inner smooth muscles (like the uterus). The womb muscles represent our capacity to hold and nourish, to feel and transmute and birth anew.

Rosemary in Summary

Working with Rosemary flower code can really show us the areas where we need to mother ourselves more by caring and nourishing our body, receiving gentle touch or a relaxing massage. It encourages us to allow time for rest, relaxation and nurturing, the space to really feel whatever is there for us. When we have not learned to hold ourselves properly, our muscles can take on the unfelt holding patterns leading to muscle tension and pain. This shows up on the surface as a deep need for soothing touch, to come back into the body (feminine) and nurture our physicality. When we are in need of a good rub or a massage - we are in need of nurturing our feminine nature of which the body is an aspect. We are in essence, in need of the energy of Rosemary. We are in need of holding ourselves with more care, love and nourishment, of allowing our feelings to flow through us, of mothering and nurturing.

Rosemary can help us relax, slow down and create more time for stillness and simply receiving. When we're not doing this enough in our lives, what can show up is many of the symptoms that Rosemary works with (muscular tension and sprains, tension or menstrual headaches, period pain and menstrual problems to name a few). Or alternately, the blockages may show up in the water vessels - the emotional realms (Rosemary stimulates the circulation and unblocks blood vessels). Its beautiful capacity to improve our awareness and presence, the memory and concentration are all descriptive of this capacity to simply be and hold space for ourselves, to not only feel, but to shine light on the inner realm.

Rosemary helps us to connect to the divine mother energy, whether we have experienced it or not. In the process, it may shine light on any wounds we have in this realm, to order to heal them.

Work with Rosemary Flower Code:
- To develop your inner capacity to feel, hold and nurture, to mother yourself.
- To work through grief of any sort in a healthy way.
- When overwhelmed with grief. For re-membering ourselves after deep grief and loss. Healthy memory.
- To support womb work, womb healing.
- To develop and heal the inner feminine or mother within.
- To recognise where mothering is out of balance.
- To develop compassion and love for all beings - independent of relationship.

As a *Mother:*
- Mother's grief, whether from loss of a child, or from the many small releases as child grows up.
- Co-dependent mother child relationships. Difficulties letting child go at the right moment, e.g.

allowing them to make own mistakes, or learn independent skills etc. Mothers who don't foster independence in children. Rosemary supports healthy release.
- Overidentification with the mother archetype - given own needs away and lost sense of self. Rosemary helps find that inner spark of self.
- Lack of healthy mothering qualities - capacity to nourish, nurture and hold space for self, child or others. Where able to nourish child but unable to nurture and nourish self.
- Difficulties holding space for emotions (in selves or others), no time or space to listen deeply and hold.

As the *Child (at any age)*
- To connect with divine mother love whether we have had it or not.
- To support feeling the emotions and grief around not having experienced healthy mother.
- To work with all mother wounds - to release grief at the humanity (rather than divine ideal) of our mothers, to feel compassion and love.
- To get in touch with our inner divine mother.
- Children subjected to co-dependent parents.

Mugwort – Great Mother

Artemisia vulgaris
Asteraceae.

Mugwort

Herbal Introduction by Pam Scott

Names and Etymology: Herb of St John, Felon Herb, Gall wood, Greenfinger, Artemis Herb, Fat Hen, Sailors Tobacco, Moogard, Muge. Initially known as Motherwort, 'Mugwort' may have originated from the word 'moughte' which translates as moth or maggot.

Mugwort is native to Europe and Asia and grows up to 3,000 metres in poor stony wasteland. It is a deciduous perennial that can grow up to about one metre. Its soft edged jagged leaves are a dark green on top and a silvery colour with fine hairs underneath. Flowers present in clusters and their colour varies from a yellowy green to a purple. Mugwort easily takes over gardens when planted directly into the ground, so might be best contained in a pot. Happily propagated from cuttings, root division and seeds, it is considered a little antisocial and is happier in gardens by itself. This could be an indication of a person who prefers their own space or needs protection from the outside world.

In many countries such as Japan, Holland and Germany, Mugwort has been used for protection. It was hung over doors and carried in pockets to protect from evil spirits, beasts and viruses. Native Americans would rub it over their bodies for protection from the dead and evil but they also considered it a valuable remedy for many ailments. Along with this protection theme, folklore says if planted in the garden then it would keep snakes away and it has been used as an antiparasitic for humans and animals. It is a great fly, mosquito and moth repellent. Other plants nearby could benefit from this repellent property, deterring bugs that may cause harm.

Mugwort seemingly has the ability to be a doorway or gatekeeper into other worlds or dimensions but also a protector from them too. Placed under the pillow with other herbs (Marjoram, Thyme and Lavender) it aids astral travelling. Prophets and psychics said they benefited from Mugwort as it induced prophetic dreams and visions.

The calming, protective energy of the plant may be beneficial when people present with sensitivities to the outside world - whether a reaction to flickering lights, loud noises, offensive or strong tastes or smells. They may have trouble switching off and could well have trouble sleeping, or their dreams are too vivid and prevent them from resting really deeply.

Mugwort balances the doorway between the left and right brain. Those needing Mugwort might have trouble putting words together, reverse words or appear to not fully comprehend what they are being told. This isn't necessarily true as their minds may be busy in other 'worlds' or they just have trouble expressing thoughts. Dyslexia and deja vu can also be associated with this herb.

Culpeper used it as a remedy for opium addiction and Dorothy Hall recommended it for reconnecting the nerve wreath in the iris if there has been an over or prolonged use of cannabis. Interestingly Mugwort leaves have been chopped and smoked to achieve a similar high, though it may have to be smoked a few times to gain the full benefit.

These days we are more familiar with mugwort as moxibustion, which is often used in conjunction with acupuncture. The heated, rolled up leaves increase circulation and therefore warm the area by bringing blood to the surface, which increases the benefit of the acupuncture needles and aids the release and flow of toxins.

Native Americans would make a poultice from the leaves for cuts, sore muscles and rheumatic conditions for the same reason and is probably why the leaves were placed inside shoes to improve stamina and endurance on long arduous walks. This circulatory effect of Mugwort has also been used to increase circulation in the pelvic area and is great to bring on a suppressed menstrual cycle, increase libido and aid fertility. Midwives have long known of these benefits and its ability to bring on uterine contractions, help release a retained afterbirth and cleanse the uterus. Mugwort is attributed to the goddess Artemis who guards the female reproductive system and any problems relating to it such as virginity, fertility and childbirth.

The bitter component in Mugwort increases bile flow and aids digestion, particularly of fatty foods and it is also helpful with food poisoning. It is a little bitter so you may want to use it sparingly when cooking or in salads. Or add some honey if making tea which is very nice after a meal or before bedtime for a guaranteed deep and restful sleep.

Constituents: Tannins, volatile oils (thujone and cineole), absinthin, bitter, santonine, potassium, magnesium and calcium.

Actions: Anti parasitic, emmenagogue, stomachic, cholagogue, nervine, diuretic, diaphoretic, digestive (fats), antispasmodic.

Contraindications: As it has a uterine stimulating effect, caution with the physical herb should be used in pregnancy.

Mugwort Teachings

The Mugwort deva is like the Great Mother who holds all seasons and phases within her. She is maiden, mother and crone in one and has the feel of a wise old grandmother - loving and kind yet sharp in that she sees all, even what you may want to hide.

As a healing herb flower code, Mugwort invites us to journey beyond the personal webs that we weave and surrender into the infinite fabric of all creation. She can help us heal blocks and wounds that prevent us from seeing clearly. The more we clear, the deeper our inner vision unfolds.

Depth

Mugwort pierces the veils with her vision and guides us to journey much deeper than the surface level. If you are willing to go beyond the superficial, Mugwort has so much to share, but she will require depth and commitment to glean just a little of the wisdom she offers. *Go deeply, give freely* she whispers. When unwilling to go deeper than the surface, Mugwort can bring out a restlessness, a superficialness that emphasises our avoidance techniques. But dive in with her and she will offer great wisdom teachings that are not for the faint hearted. Seeing our patterning can be confronting, hence the need for commitment and willingness when you work with her.

As a plant categorised under the Moon, Mugwort supports inner vision, dreaming and insight, and encourages us to look into the unseen realms to gain greater understanding. You can see some of her lunar plant signatures in the silvery backs of the leaves; the tiny, unpretentious moonlike flowers; and the arrow like leaves reminiscent of the moon goddess, Artemis' arrows, to name a few.

Protection

Mugwort is one of three master protectors of the plant world. Worn on the person as a protection amulet, or burned to purify spaces are some external methods of use over the years. When we are in need of energetic protection, wearing Mugwort can be very helpful. On a deeper level, Mugwort will show you how to protect yourself from the inside out by improving the integrity of your own weaving (more on that below). By *really* taking responsibility for your energetic field, external amulets will not be necessary, but until that time, she is a loving and protective guide through the realms.

Mugwort is especially useful for the mucky energies of substance abuse, and is used particularly to antidote the overuse of cannabis (in any form), which loosens the integrity of our weave. In the current overuse phase of 'cannabis is good for everything,' Mugwort is a much needed herb to reweave the threads and see beyond the illusion and smoke and mirrors reflections.

Maiden Mother Crone. Great Mother of All

Mugwort carries the essence of the *Great Mother of All*. She is maiden mother and crone all at once, holding all of the seasons within her field. As mother of all children (including spirit babies who she returns home), she cares for all equally and makes sure the quiet ones don't slip through the cracks and become overshadowed. All beings are her children and none more important than another. She is an important teacher of group space weaving in this sense.

Ancestry

Meeting Mugwort for most is like coming home to a long lost, yet familiar great grandmother. Having witnessed countless people work with her, it appears that she shows up in the ancestral guises and cultures that relate to the person. In a sense she taps us into our ancestry. Her feeling is so familiar to us as it speaks through our own lineages. Slowly I came to understand that much more deeply, Mugwort taps us into the *Great Mother* - the mother of all, who is an ancestor to everyone. The great cosmic mother.

Mugwort acts as a guide to journey along our ancestral lines to eventually find at the centre the great mother weaving the threads of destiny and holding all within her tapestry. Like a spider at the centre of the great cosmic web of life. She will support us to journey along the threads of our DNA, the threads woven by our ancestors in order to unravel and reweave aspects that no longer serve.

Vision and Journeying

Mugwort is a journey plant. It can help you see the unseen, gain a greater perspective of things, and protect you along the way. Whether this is through dreaming, astral travel or shamanic journey, Mugwort can help you fly beyond the smoke and mirrors of your own version of reality, out beyond your personal matrix and into the greater cosmic web.

Mugwort is like a power animal in plant form - she guides us through other realms along the threads of our intention and protects us as we travel these webs.

Mugwort is a herb of vision. A superficial look at her and she will simply mirror your reflections. "Smoke and mirrors" delusions, projections and illusions are all an aspect of her shadow side. Basically, you'll see what you want to see. Think crystal ball fortune telling in the hazy smoke of Mugwort in order to fool or create a smokescreen. Or the hazy grey aura of cannabis use that keeps us in denial while under the illusion we are "connected" (one of cannabis' homeopathic rubrics).

On the flip side, Mugwort can take you beyond the reflections of your own projected world to see a bigger picture. But before we do that, we need to heal any wounds we have to seeing. There can be so many reasons we keep our inner vision/third eye closed and not wanting to see. Maybe our ancestry once used our inner sight for personal gain; or despite 'seeing' could do nothing to change an outcome; maybe we missed seeing something that had huge consequences and have never forgiven ourselves. The different possibilities of past traumas woven into our psyche and the collective psyche are endless.

The first layer of Mugwort is to heal and unwind these wounds in order to take the next step.... to awaken the inner seer, the eye who sees all. This is not necessarily a quick process! Unravelling these threads can take time and a fair amount of letting go of previous held notions.

The Great Weaver

Mugwort is like a master weaver of the tapestry of destiny we live in. Tapping into Mugwort is to tap into the threads of the web we are woven into, of which there are many layers.

When you first work with her, most probably you'll visit your personal weave. Tapping into the threads of our weave, we can begin to unravel who we are, and if we choose, to reweave certain aspects. We may find threads running our life that come from deep in our ancestry, our current life, or other versions of ourselves/lives, of wounds or old beliefs, designed to protect yet that are now holding us back. For our personal threads are the weaving of our DNA. They carry rich veins of blessings, along with countless traumas, vows, memories and seeds built from the past. Not all of these will be valuable or relevant in the present and yet they may still be running us. Mugwort takes us back to the areas that may need repair or reweaving so that we can choose to reveal the rich gems in our bloodlines rather than be ruled by ancient traumas.

It is the threads of our lives that create our future. *Who we are in this moment now - whatever we are feeling, believing and subtly perceiving as truth is creating not only our future but our past!* This is another Mugwort teaching. When we become conscious of how we are really seeing the world, we can unravel and reweave it in this very moment. Again, Mugwort works DEEPLY, in the dark caves of our underground consciousness and subconsciousness. But this is where the root of our woven web lies. Like a spider that sits at the centre of the web that it has woven from its inner world, so are we the creators of our destiny - from our inner workings, whether they are conscious or unconscious.

Unravelling and reweaving is a big part of Mugwort's vision medicine.

Mugwort is akin to the Norns or the Weavers of Destiny, the Three Fates of mythology - those who spin the thread of life, weave its tapestry and cut the final thread of life. The triple goddess. maiden, mother and crone all at once, she knows intimately all parts of the cycle are valuable - including death. Mugwort can take us along these threads to meet the Weaver of our Destiny and rework the tapestry of our lives. She will not do the healing for you, but she will show you the threads that may need work and support you in the process.

The womb. Warmth

The womb is the physical manifestation of our inner mother, the cauldron that holds space for the process of creation. In a fractal sense, the physical womb is the smaller mother, the personal weaver of our realm akin to Rosemary; while Mugwort, as Great Mother of the Cosmos, relates to the cosmic womb. The great cauldron of creation. In this sense, we can also think of her for when we create group cauldrons, collective womb spaces when we work in sacred circle with other people.

Mugwort has a known action on the muscles and possibly its true seat of action is not the womb itself, but the underlying seat of the womb - the pelvic floor. Just as the Great Mother is mother to all mothers, the pelvic basin underlies the womb itself. The pelvic bowl is an even greater vessel of receiving, which holds space for the womb, which in turn holds space for new life.

Mugwort has a theme of integrity - in relation to the way we walk in the world, in the way we weave our world, but also the integrity of this foundational bowl of the pelvic floor, the *seat of life*. If it is too tight, then things don't land properly. If it is too loose, then all falls through. The integrity of our weave is important. The integrity of our pelvic bowl muscles affects the womb and its capacity to weave, create, receive, hold and release.

One of Mugwort's 'seat of influences' is in the muscles. Spasms, epilepsy, tics and twitches throughout the body are within her scope. There is a feeling of muscles contracting as if squeezing out old energy within her field, as if releasing stuck energy, clearing the old, but on a muscular level. Mugwort seems to reach into weaker areas of the body where memories and tension are storied, to help release them. In the release comes the movement, like spasms as the body reworks itself (another version of Yarrow's processing through the body). It brings a sense of much needing to be cleared and moved through the muscles.

Mugwort also has a theme of warmth. It is warming and drying and useful for cold, damp conditions. Moxa or burning a few dried leaves is a great application.

Mugwort in Summary

Mugwort is a journey plant. To work with her teachings, is to be taken along the threads of your own weaving, so that you can unravel and reweave parts of your life that are no longer serving. She will open your eyes to aspects of yourself that are working out of fear or from outdated beliefs. She can take you along the threads of your ancestors to the source of the tension, to what requires unravelling so as to bring consciousness to this pattern so that you can choose whether you want to keep creating from that place. She helps you *see* your deep inner workings and the way you are creating.

These old patterns and outdated beliefs are held in the body, frozen. Mugwort warms and gently encourages us to unravel frozen threads that hold old patterns, beliefs and traumas. There may be corresponding muscular release as the shift occurs, which is the body's way of squeezing out the old.

Once we go beyond the weavings or mirrors of our own personal truth, we can travel further into a larger truth. To rest in the arms of the cosmic mother and to trust the weaving of the great web of life that contains all beings within it. While we create our reality based on what we are projecting onto the world via our subconscious and conscious threads, there is also a bigger truth - that we are also just one thread in the whole fabric of creation.

Mugwort will first help you to find and unravel unhealthy weavings in your own tapestry and the way you are creating your world. Then, when and if you are ready, Mugwort can help you travel further into a deeper and greater reality or perspective of the world. She can help you to tune into your original nature, the gold veins within your DNA. And then to travel beyond into the cosmic realms, to see far - to support you to astral travel, remote view etc. But it is important to do the clearing work first. For seeing further brings great responsibility and the need for much integrity. The deeper into our unconscious realm or the farther we travel into new realms (which are the same thing), the more compassion is needed. This is not something to do in an instant as it requires deeper inner work, but the Great Mother herb is here to support you and guide you if you are ready.

As *protector*, Mugwort flower code will help you hold your ground steadily and maintain integrity when boundaries are being challenged. With consciousness, she can be sought to clear and reweave the integrity back into a space, person or place which has been transgressed. At the core of the teachings of Mugwort, is the lesson that your *integrity* in each moment ripples through the web of creation, creating not just the future but the past. It is from the present moment that your weaving unfolds. And it is from this moment, that all can change.

As *Great Mother*, Mugwort reminds us that every being within the fabric of creation is as important as every other being. That the tiny invisible threads (and creatures) are as important to the great web as the loud, big and dramatic. Herein lies a warning: to take notice of the subtle and give it equal measure as the loud and dramatic in your world. To be able to see *more of the strands* of creation, is one of the gifts of Mugwort, yet it comes with the coexisting necessity to grow your capacity for compassion. The deeper into our unconscious world we see, the more compassion is required.

Working consciously with Mugwort helps us journey further and see more of the threads of the cosmos; it supports the healing of blocks to this deeper vision and dreaming, to see beyond the illusions of our reflected belief systems to a greater truth.

It is a powerful dreaming plant in all senses of the word as it helps us to remember and amplify our dreams and astral travel; to see how we are dreaming our world into being and hence make choices around what we want to create; in removing blocks to our vision/dreaming (with conscious work); offers protection as we journey forth into other realms; strengthens integrity by working with the threads of our personal dreaming; and works on the integrity of pelvic floor muscles, the seat of the womb and our creative powers.

Mugwort won't do the work for you, but with consciousness, she will assist you to see more clearly, dream and create with more integrity and protect you along the way.

Work with Mugwort flower code:
- To see your patterning and how it affects your world.
- To protect you as you delve into your personal weaving and the cosmic collective dreaming should you venture so far.
- Assistance and protection with dreaming, journeying and astral travelling.
- To travel beneath the surface, beneath collective and personal versions of history to a greater truth.
- To clear and see beyond smoke and mirrors, veils and programmes - of your own or others.
- To work *safely* with ancestors for healing and discovering the gifts you hold.
- To clear and reweave old patterning.
- To recognise the power of the small, subtle and invisible rather than give all attention to the loud, visible and obvious.
- To work on integrity and boundaries.
- To develop deeper aspects of holding space - through integrity and compassion for *all* beings.

Postcript

If nature is a library, then each plant species is like a book. Each plant contains a rich stellium of teachings and themes.

You'll have noticed no doubt, that there are many thematic overlaps with the healing herbs in this book. Each of these common herbs is so collective and global that they reach far and wide not only on the Earth, but within our psyches.

The closer we get to the core or 'spirit' medicine of each plant, the more we'll find the commonality. Connection, disconnection, blocks, processing emotions, these are some of the themes we've visited via many different plant teachers (and that you'll encounter in many more). The trick then is to find the clothing, the soul medicine that matches your own needs.

Which 'disconnection' is ripe for you to work with? The separative wounds of Calendula or the out of body traumas of Yarrow? Do your obstacles to processing have the flavor of Dandelion (and its addictions), Yarrow (and its trauma, suppression, laziness or procrastination), Rosemary (big emotional feels), or Chamomile (overwhelm and external distraction)? The more you begin to play with the soul medicine of plants, the more they will guide and surprise you.

May the medicine of the herb devas be with you on your journey!

Gratitude

This book wouldn't be as rich with plant wisdom if I was doing it alone - big thanks to all my herbal colleagues and students, fellow plant whisperers and earth guardians whose trusting dives into the soulful medicine of the flower codes has kept them ever growing - both expanding and concentrating at once the themes of each herb. It is such an honour to be working alongside the plant spirits with you.

Deep gratitude to Pam and Michelle for their awesome and unique contributions to the Materia Medica sections of this book.

And special thanks to Kassey Weaver and Mikala Maloney for their contributions on Calendula's soul medicine during our spagyric alchemy and permission to share some of their words directly.

And of course, I'm ever so grateful to the herbs, flower fairies and hidden folk for their support and the wisdom they continue to teach me day in and day out.

Resources

For information about the *Shamanic Herbalism Flower Codes Training* - a path of plant spirit teachings, flower medicine and embodied herbalism that will deepen your connection with nature and support your soul to bloom, visit www.wildflowerwalker.com

The Flower Code essences can be purchased at www.theflowercodes.com or www.wildflowerwalker.com

Book 1: Sacred Birth of *The Flower Codes* series: *Plant Spirit Teachings for your Soul to Blossom* can be found at www.wildflowerwalker.com or at all your online bookstores.

About the Authors

Michelle Carnochan

Michelle is a professionally qualified Homeopath, Herbalist, Integrative Womb Hara Massage Therapist, Pre and Perinatal Educator, and a former Doula. Her praxis is much informed by preservation of the wisdom of the Old Ways, and in her spare time she reads the runes and writes about plant whispering, primal imprints, ancestral healing, and the myths and magick that shape us at:
 changelingdreamtime.substack.com

Pam Scott

Pam began her herbal journey in the late 1990's. She completed a 3-year Herbal Medicine Diploma course with Kim Dudley at the Hierophant in Canberra and continued her studies there for another couple of years participating in some Herbal extension lectures and a year of Homeopathy with Tim Thomas. After another 2 years at The Dorothy Hall College of Herbal Medicine, she received an Advanced Diploma of Herbal Medicine. Through this course she also studied Nutrition, Iridology, Astrology and Bach Flower Therapy. She has also spent extended periods of time over the last twenty years studying with renowned American Herbalist, Matthew Wood. In 2013 she received a Diploma in Biochemic Therapy, and still uses these Tissue Salts as an integral part of her prescription protocol.

For over 15 years, Pam was the Practitioner at Canberra's popular Health/Wholefoods shop, Mountain Creek Wholefoods where she was able to help people with a wide variety of dietary advice and many other issues and ailments.

She also worked at The Hierophant for a few years dispensing Herbal and Homeopathic Medicines. She has also studied Swedish Massage, Kinesiology, Kinergy and has a strong interest and love for Jungian Psychology after taking her own journey with a Jungian Analyst, exploring dreams and symbols for over 4 years.

She now lives on the South Coast. With such a diversity of modalities and experience, Pam can weave a wellness prescription for your well-being.
www.weavingwellness.com.au

Heidi Wedd

Heidi has been walking the plant spirit path for almost 30 years. With herbalism, homeopathy, and plant alchemy (spagyrics) as early companions in the late 90's, midwifery and shamanism came a little later. After years of being fascinated listening to the teachings of plants, she has since taught hundreds of people how to deepen their connection with nature, hear the whispers of plants and inspire living in greater harmony with self and nature at the Wildflowerwalker Plant Spirit Herbalism & Flower Shamanism School.

Acclaimed author of Wild Flower Walker: A Pilgrimage to Nature on the Bibbulmun Track and *The Flower Codes: Plant Spirit Teachings for your Soul to Blossom, Bk 1: Sacred*

Birth, she continues to teach, write and be on an ever evolving journey guided by plants.
 www.theflowercodes.com
 www.wildflowerwalker.com

Book 1 in *The Flower Codes* series: **Sacred Birth**.

Activating the Language of Flowers

Imagine a world where everyone has the opportunity to thrive and blossom to their full soul potential. Imagine a culture that realises personal blooming not only benefits the whole but enhances everyone's capacity to shine. Could flowers hold a key?

In *The Flower Codes,* messages and teachings received in conversation with the plant devas, are combined with grounded herbal wisdom, historical knowledge and years of herbal experience to reveal the power of flowers to awaken, heal and guide us to remember and embody our blossoming self. In the first book of the series, the three flowers that contain the ancient encoding for sacred birth are explored in depth - for the first step in birthing a Sacred Earth lies in our inner transformation.

"...takes you straight into the essence of the flower's soul and widens your perspective on the consciousness that plants contain. Can't wait for the next instalment."

Available at www.wildflowerwalker.com or all online bookstores

Wild Flower Walker:
A Pilgrimage to Nature on the Bibbulmun Track.

WILD FLOWER WALKER
A Pilgrimage to Nature on the Bibbulmun Track

Heidi Wedd

"Absolutely loved it. I couldn't put it down - the journey, the words, the inner knowing and learning is inspiring. It is a book I will gift to loved ones." *J.M*

She imagined the bliss of walking for weeks on end, the silence of being alone and the space to commune more deeply with nature spirits. But will the nonstop challenges of reality hinder her dream of a deeper union with nature?

This is the engaging story of a young woman solo hiking 1000km through Western Australia's wildflower filled bush. On a quest to listen more deeply to nature and despite a myriad of challenges and adventures along the way, what unfolds is a reweaving and reconnection into the very heart of nature.

Find yourself within nature's intricate tapestry as you walk the Bibbulmun track alongside her.

Available at www.wildflowerwalker.com or all online bookstores.

www.ingramcontent.com/pod-product-compliance
Lightning Source LLC
Chambersburg PA
CBHW071719020426
42333CB00017B/2329